SEAFARING

Captain Gerard H. Bassett

ATHENA PRESS
LONDON

SEAFARING
Copyright © Captain Gerard H. Bassett 2002

All Rights Reserved

ISBN 1 930493 87 8

First Published 2002 by
ATHENA PRESS
Queen's House, 2 Holly Road
Twickenham TW1 4EG

Printed for Athena Press

SEAFARING

This book is dedicated with many fond memories to my many friends and shipmates who sailed with me and the experiences we shared together in time of war and peace during my seagoing career.

ABOUT THE AUTHOR

Captain Gerard H. Bassett was born in Salem, Ma. He attended schools in Salem and Providence, where his family moved to C later, and spent six months in a CCC camp in Palisades, Colorado.

After returning home, he decided to go to sea, following the footsteps of an uncle who also went to sea. Captain's elder brother, who ran away from home at the age of fifteen, went to sea too and spent most of his life there.

After receiving seamen's papers, Captain Bassett went to New York and got a trip card with a union and got a seagoing job on Hog Island Ship. He sailed all through World War II and retired as a sailor.

In recognition of his services rendered, he received the American Defense Ribbon (pre-war), Combat Bar with four stars, Atlantic War Zone Ribbon, Pacific War Zone Ribbon, Mediterranean and Middle East War Zone Ribbon, World War II Victory Ribbon and the Vietnam Service Ribbon.

Captain Bassett, who lived in Rhode Island till his retirement and moved to Homosassa, Florida later, is presently a member of the American Council of Masters Mariners, the National Maritime Historical Society and Masters, Mates and Pilots Union.

The Sea

*How I love to gaze upon her mysterious and ever changing face
from a smooth placid sparkling with sunlight reflecting off the
surface like thousands of flashing diamonds;
To a roaring, raging, smashing fury destroying everything in its
path, smashing steel as if it were paper with mountainous waves
wearing down mountains to beach sand,
From an emerald and freezing cold and forbidding Arctic and
Antartic seas to the warm cobalt blue and inviting tropical seas.*

*How many secrets do her depths hold?
How many treasures, bodies and ships have they swallowed up—
and have never spit them up?*

*Under her surface the ocean is teeming with life.
It has an unending fascination and attraction for us who go to sea,
and at times is fatal for us, and has an unending grip upon us
which is almost unbreakable.*

*I have gazed upon the sea in all her moods, and I am still
fascinated by the wonder of it all.*

Gerald H. Bassett

Contents

Chapter I

SEAFARING

I was born in the old seaport of Salem, Massachusetts. My parents rented a house on the seashore and I was fascinated by the sea. I spent endless hours on the beach alone studying all sorts of marine life that washed up on the beach. The sea itself intrigued me and has held me in its grip all of my life.

One cannot explain this phenomenon unless one has been to sea and sailed on it, as it is a life completely different from living on land.

I shall try to open that window to show you that going to sea is one of the world's oldest professions. In Europe it is considered an honorable profession, but in the United States, if you went to sea you were considered a bum by the public. Yet it was highly regarded in the early years of our nation and seafarers were highly thought of.

Shipping was the foundation of all the great fortunes in the United States. Before the railroads were built almost all goods were shipped by ship, coastwise. We had coastwise ships until World War II. It was never revived after the war due to the economics of the trade and to the fact that the shipping companies did not want to risk their capital in coastwise shipping.

There were over four hundred ships engaged in the coastwise trade at the beginning of World War II. Some of the companies engaged in the coastwise trade were C D Mallory, Merchant Miner, Bull Line, Cuban Mail Line, Agawi, and I am almost forgetting the united fruit lines, or banana lines, as we used to call them, and Sea Train, which ran box cars to Cuba from Florida and Lukenbach which our seamen called broken back because of the double booms and rigging at each hatch. They also had six or seven or more hatches on their ship in order to be more efficient in loading and discharging cargo simultaneously.

Our government discovered that the Sea Train ships made good tank carriers as they loaded them with tanks and sent them around the Cape of Good Hope and up through the Red Sea to the British forces in North Africa who were losing the war against Rommel. This was because the Mediterranean was controlled by the German and Italian air forces. Convoys with supplies were being destroyed by them. The British suffered tremendous losses in trying to supply their troops to the Island of Malta. Those tanks delivered by the Sea Train ships helped to stem the war in North Africa.

The earth's surface comprises seventy-one percent of water and man soon discovered that the easiest way to transport material was over water.

The earliest record of transportation through water is from the Egyptians, who shipped grains and vegetables up the Nile River. They also sent stone blocks while building the Pyramids.

The Egyptians soon learned that sails propelled loaded ships faster than oars. The Egyptians also ventured out into the Eastern Mediterranean to establish trade.

The Phoenicians were great seafarers who sailed all over the Mediterranean and established trade routes as far as Gaul and Great Britain. The ships they built were also the first to have enclosed the poop, also called the stern, and the forepeak, which were called thus after castle and forecastle. This name remains even today as a term for seamen's living quarters.

The ancient Greeks were also seafarers. They supplied to their colonies in North Africa and brought back grains and other raw materials as Greece did not have much arable land for growing crops.

The ancient Romans were not seafarers in the beginning as they were a nation of farmers and artisans, but had to learn as their empire grew and they had to supply their garrisons, relieve their troops and also carry on trade with their colonies.

The Vikings were great seafarers but their main purpose was raiding, pillaging, stealing and killing. They plundered Europe as far east as Italy and as far west as Iceland, Greenland and eastern America.

About these early seafarers, we have no clue as to whether they were free men or slaves or as to what kind of shelter they had aboard the ships. Most likely, all they had was a pile of straw and some sort of covering blanket or rags and possibly an awning to keep off the rain and spray them with water in jugs. They probably ate some sort of bread or grains. They had a rough life.

The Venetians were the greatest traders and seafarers that the Mediterranean had ever seen. They traded all over the place and bought and sold spices and silk products, which were carried over to the Middle East from the Far East by Arab traders in dhows.

The Venetians were also the first to provide shelter for their seamen. We know that they were free men as the Venetians did not have any slaves.

The Venetians made money from carrying the Crusaders and pilgrims to and from the holy land. They reached their peak about A.D. 1100.

The Portuguese were also great navigators due to Prince Henry, who had done a lot of research on navigation. The Portuguese commenced sailing down the West Coast of Africa farther and farther until they found their way around the Cape of Good Hope and up the East Coast of Africa and reached the island of Mauritania, from there to the west coast of India. They landed at Goa and set up a trading post and a colony to trade with the Indians.

After the discovery of the new world, all the other maritime nations set out to grab their share of the new world and its supposed treasures. They all found new colonies to reap all the wealth found there.

The nations in the race included the French, the Dutch, the English and the Spanish, who were already there. Conflicts and wars followed as they all wanted to control all the territory and not share it, but bring back all the wealth to their home countries.

The English were great navigators and discovered a lot of new territory because of men like Drake and Cook.

All the land that was discovered was by seafarers and all of that was charted by oceans, shoals and reefs. All of the unknown world. The world would not have been discovered if it were not for seafarers and the hard life they shared in order to sail to these lands and the dangers they faced in these unknown oceans and lands. The world should be thankful to these brave seafarers for all the discoveries they made over the centuries.

As the American colonies grew, the need for shipping also grew simultaneously. So the American colonies began to design and build their own ships that were superior in design and speed than the British. The British deeply resented this.

All merchant ships during the age of sail were armed with cannons and firearms as the world was a dangerous place and everyone needed to be protected.

In the revolutionary war, there was no navy. Armed merchantmen comprised the Navy. There were armed privateers commissioned by the Continental Congress, who captured a lot of English merchantmen as well as British men of war and that brought the ire of the owners of those ships on them. The US Navy does not like to admit this, but there were always merchant ships before the navy, which were founded to protect a nation's merchant fleet, which was the economic backbone of maritime nations.

The British Navy was always desperately in need of seamen for their fleet and took to taking seaman off American merchant ships, claiming that they were British subjects and including them into their navy. This brought a howl of protest from the shipowners as it was interfering with Americans' trade. This practice brought on the war of 1812. The British Navy also had press gangs, who wandered along the waterfront, entered the pubs and took anyone who looked fit enough aboard the warships and pressed them into service.

The Barbary pirates who began to seize American merchant ships off their coast and holding their crew for ransom irritated the shipowners and the American public and government began a shipbuilding program to fight these pirates. Thus we built the USS Constitution and the USS Constellation, which heralded the real birth of the US Navy. Again, it was for the protection of American merchant fleet because shipping was their lifeblood.

The USS Constitution and USS Constellation were built in 1798 and were the first ships built for the US Navy. The USS Constitution earned its nickname Old Ironsides while fighting the British as the British shells bounced off of hull as if it was made of iron.

The clipper ships were a great improvement in living conditions for the seafarers who sailed on them, but the work was hard. They worked six hours on and six hours off but they could also be called any time and at any hour to take in or raise more sails, depending on the weather. There were days when they did not get much rest.

Can you imagine eighteen people living in one room, sleeping and eating, drying clothes with no light except one lantern, always damp, the food brought to the forecastle in a bucket, each seaman had to furnish his own cup, plate and eating utensils.

Also, there was no fresh water with which to bathe or shave, only salt water. The fresh water was stored in wooden barrels and soon got stale and rancid and hot water was almost unknown unless the sailors could steal some from the galley, but if they were caught they would be punished. The food was mostly corned beef or pork that also soon got rancid and mouldy. The bread was as hard as a rock but preserved well. They also had potatoes, onions, and other vegetables until they rotted. It was a very hard life but men continued to go to sea and returned time after time.

The ship's master often brought chicken, pigs or sheep for his own use.

The ship's master, the chief mate, and the second mate lived aft and they each had a cabin but they worked the same as the crew—six hours on watch and six hours off. They had much better living conditions.

There were people who preyed on seamen in those days. They either drugged them or got them drunk and delivered to ships for a price as ships were always short-handed when they went out to sea. With no recourse for anyone, often the seamen's boarding houses made them sign outrageous allotments to them from the very ship's master so that by the time the voyage was over they had very little money left.

Conditions got progressively worse through the years until Richard Henry Dana wrote his book *Two Years Before The Mast*. It exposed the terrible conditions aboard American merchant ships. He became a champion for seamen and became their attorney before the courts. In 1791, Congress revised the law, setting up shipping articles and shipping commissioners who oversaw the signing on of seamen to witness that they signed of their own free will. Also, the shipping articles had to be posted and it stated the amounts of daily rations each man had to receive. That put an end to starvation and shanghaiing of seamen.

To this day, ships must carry lime juice, as the British had found that lime juice prevented scurvy. That is how they got the nickname limeys and seafarers still call them by this name.

Sailing ships made a great improvement when they built sailing ships with hulls of iron. It created much stronger and watertight vessels. It also created better quarters for seamen.

But with the advent of steam-propelled vessels, who could stay on a schedule? Some survived until the early twentieth century by hauling grains and coal. The most beautiful ships that were ever built were left to rot at docks all over the world, except for a few that were saved by the National Maritime Historical Society, which should be praised for its effort and work in finding returning to the United States these beautiful ships for other generations to see and admire. Such people should be acknowledged.

I have admired these ships all my life and continue to do so. They were things of beauty, which will never be seen again.

The sea routes that were developed by sailing ships' masters are still followed to this day by modern ships. A great change came in the certification and licensing of ships' crews after the fire and the grounding of the SS *Moro Castle*, a passenger ship off the coast of NJ. There were claims that some of the crew deserted the ship and went ashore in the lifeboats and did not aid the passengers to evacuate the ship. This caused uproar in the press. So in 1937, Congress changed the marine laws on certification and licensing crew members, also requiring that 90% of the crew be American citizens. The US Congress revamped the steamboat inspectors who inspected ships and gave the test to seamen. I heartily agreed with these new tests so that the competence of seafarers would be raised.

The 1930s was a time of great struggle that continued until World War II. Seamen were so frustrated by the steamship companies' refusal to upgrade their living and working conditions that they began to organize unions to fight for their rights. This was a very violent period in the maritime industry. The unions began strikes against the steamship companies as they had refused to recognize them. The steamship companies, in turn, hired so-called goon squads to terrorize the seamen walking the picket lines, attacking them with clubs, chains, brass knuckles and also with guns. Scores of seamen were injured and killed by these goon squads. Finally, the United States government stepped in and forced the companies to negotiate with the unions and sign an agreement to end these brutal strikes.

Ships' crews are divided into three departments: deck, engine and stewards. The deck department consisted of a chief mate, second mate, third mate, a bosun, a deck maintainer, six ABS, and three OS.

The engine department consisted of a chief engineer, first assistance engineer, second assistance engineer, third assistance engineer, three oilers, three firemen water-tenders, two wipers and a deck engineer on freighters or a pump man on tankers.

The stewards department consisted of a chief steward, chief cook, second cook and baker, a third cook, a galley man, a pantry man, two mess men, and a bedroom utility.

The ship's master, or captain (as his license says Master, not Captain) is the master of the ship and has overall command of everyone on board. He oversees everyone and his word is law. Even when a pilot boards a ship, the pilot directs the ship into the harbor under the authority of the ship's master. He is also responsible for the entire ship and his actions are also binding on the shipowners.

The captain must also make out the payroll, handle the slop chest, which is a little store of clothing, toilet articles, cigarettes, tobacco, and candy. A slop chest aboard a ship is required by law. He is allowed to make a ten percent profit. He supervises the navigation and the ship's position. He is on call twenty-four hours a day. He keeps the official logbook, as required by law. He must inspect the entire ship and hold fire and boat drills weekly. There are several logbooks aboard the ship. The official logbook kept by the master, the deck logbook kept on bridge regarding the ship's position, temperatures, clouds, wind directions and velocity and the noon position of the ship along with the cargo operations while in port and events that happened aboard.

The weather reports are sent by radio message daily to the US Weather Bureau. The official logbook also records deaths, births and marriages. The ship's master must make out a crew list, custom and immigration forms, crew customs declarations and different forms for the ship's entry into foreign ports as well as slop chest inventories. As they say, the buck stops with him.

The chief mate stands the four-to-eight watch at sea. He takes star sights morning and night to obtain the ship's position if the weather permits, as star sights are the most reliable of all positioning systems. He is also responsible for the loading and discharging of all cargo and the upkeep of the ship's exterior and some of the interior, excluding the engine spaces and the galley and steward department, as each department paints their own quarters.

The second mate is responsible for maintaining navigating charts and publications and making corrections that are sent out by US Hydrographic Office. He also keeps the ship's clocks wound and corrected. He is also responsible for cleaning and maintaining the Gyrocompass, which is located in the chart room.

The third mate is responsible for daily winding of the ship's chronometer and for checking its rate by a radio signal from the US Naval Observatory in Arlington that sends a timed signal, which the ship's radio operator receives and sends up to a jack in the chart room. There, the third mate listens and notices if the chronometer is fast or slow as Greenwich time and enters it in the chronometer rate book which is kept in the chart room. Also, he must take sights and plot them on the chart and must take azimuth to see if there is any error in the compasses and enter it into the azimuth book. All watch officers must take at least one azimuth bearing during their watch. The third mate also reads the ship's draft after docking and before sailing and enters it into the deck logbook.

These duties evolved over the centuries from two-mate sailing ships to three-mate powered ships as these duties were done by the two mates on a sailing ship.

The bridge equipment consists of two radar sets, side band radio to communicate with other ships, a magnetic compass, a hydraulic steering system with a wooden wheel, a magnetic compass in a binnacle, a gyrocompass with a repeater on each wing of the bridge—port and starboard—to take bearings, and a telephone that connects the whole ship. There is an automatic steering system called an iron mike that steers the ship. A telegraph is connected to the engine room and all engine orders are made by this system. There's a flashlight, two sets of binoculars, controls for a searchlight that is on the flying bridge, and running lights switches. Flag boxes contain all the signal flags and flags of all nations. The most used is the B flag. It is red and means there are explosives on board or the ship is loading or discharging explosives at night when a single red light is shown.

The Q flag is yellow and exhibited when there is contagious disease aboard and the ship is quarantined. No one is allowed on or oft. The H flag flown while approaching port means the ship requires a pilot. After the pilot boards the ship, the P flag is flown, meaning a pilot is aboard. The chart room equipment consists of the following equipment: a chart table with drawers that contain charts that cover the world, a fathometer for taking soundings of the depth of the water under the keel, the chronometer case with the chronometer in it, a loran set to take loran bearings for navigation, and all the other nautical publications. The ship's captain and the mates own their own sextants, and also a radio direction finder to take bearings on lighthouses as they also send out radio signals as well as flashing lights.

When the ship is docking or undocking, the master is on the bridge commanding the ship. The third mate is on the bridge assisting him, ringing the telegraph to change the vessel speed that the master commands and repeating steering orders and seeing that they are carried out by the helmsman. The chief mate is on the bow and the second mate is on the stern with the deck crew split up half forward and the other half on the stern. The chief mate always goes forward on the bow when it is necessary to drop the anchor, or heave it up, and has the bosun and the current watch with him.

The bosun is the deck department foreman. He reports to the

chief mate every morning and gets his orders for the work that the chief mate wants to be completed that day. The bosun, in turn, puts the seamen to work, giving them the tools or equipment or paint, whatever is needed. The bosun is also the storekeeper and keeps inventory of the deck department supplies. He is a day worker.

The deck maintenance is also a day worker. Their hours are eight to five. The deck maintenance also works under the bosun. There are six able bodies and three ordinary seamen divided into three watches—eight to twelve, twelve to four and four to eight, i.e., A.M. and P.M. They steer the ship and work on the deck under the bosun for two hours and work for two hours on the bridge when the ship is being steered by the automatic helm or iron mike, as we call it. During the night watches, they take turns steering and keeping a lookout on the bow of the ship, reporting to the bridge all lights observed by ringing the ship's bell on the bow—one bell for the starboard, two bells for the port side, and three bells for dead ahead. After daylight, the four-to-eight watch cleans the bridge windows and the bridge itself.

The radio officer works eight hours out of twelve. His hours are flexible in order to receive any messages at radio traffic time. He also gets the time signal in the morning for the third mate to check the ship's chronometer. He sends and receives messages for the ship's master, receives weather reports and sends out weather reports to the US weather bureau. There is an emergency alarm in the radio room in his room. An SOS will trigger it off so that he can respond to it.

The engine department is composed of a chief engineer, a first engineer, and each second and third engineers, three oilers, three firemen, water tenders, and also two wipers.

The chief engineer is in charge of whole engine department. He is responsible for maintaining all of the ship's machinery, including the deck winches. The first engineer carries out the repairs as ordered by the chief engineer. The second engineer is responsible for maintaining the ships boilers while the third engineer is responsible for the electric system and generators. The fireman and water tenders perform a combination job of keeping the boilers operating. The oilers make rounds oiling the auxiliary machinery, including the ship's shaft. The wipers do cleaning up, painting and other tasks as ordered by the first engineer.

Freighters and tankers have the same crew members except that freighters have an additional member—a deck engineer who maintains the deck machinery and the cargo winches.

He is under the first engineer. Tankers carry a pump man who maintains the deck winches but also operates the cargo pumps and maintains them. He works under two bosses—the first engineer when repairing deck winches or the cargo pumps. When the ship is cleaning tanks or discharging cargo, he is under the chief mate's direction.

The steward's department consists of a chief steward, a chief cook, a second cook and baker, a third cook and galley man, a pantry man and dishwasher, a crew mess man, a saloon mess man and a steward's utility man.

The chief steward is in charge of the stewards department. He keeps inventory of his supplies as all department heads have to. He also makes out the daily menu and supervises the work of all his members.

The chief cooks all the meats and vegetables. The second cook and baker bake bread and pastries and help the chief cook with breakfast and dinner. The third cook and galley man bring up supplies for the day's cooking, prepare vegetables for meals and wash all the pots and pans and other utensils used in the cooking.

The pantry man prepares salads and washes the dishes of the crew and saloon mess rooms. The crew's mess man serves the crew's meals and keeps the mess room clean. The saloon mess man does the same in the ship's officers' saloon. The steward's utility man cleans and makes the officers' beds. Everyone aboard the ship receives two sheets, two bath towels, two hand towels, two pillowcases, two bars of soap, and one box of soap powder, and one carton of safety matches every week.

In the days before the ships were equipped with washing machines and dryers, we were given two bars of washing yellow soap as we had to scrub our clothes by hand and dry them in the space above the ship's boilers. The ship's engineers hated that practice as clothes often fell on to the tops of the boilers and sometimes caught fire which had to be put out by the engine crew.

All seamen carry sewing kits and some have flat irons. As we all knew how to repair and wash and iron our clothes, this tradition has been carried on for centuries.

Seamen also still carry sheath knives as one never knows when one can become entangled in a line and should be able to cut oneself free to save one's life or possibly save a limb.

Seamen themselves have their own code of ethics about keeping the living quarters and themselves very clean. You may see ships that look rusty on the outside but the interior is kept very clean. Seamen have learned over the centuries that cleanliness has prevented the spread of disease.

Seamen do not tolerate a thief. They have been known to have fallen overboard and never been found. One does not pry into the personal life of others aboard. If they do disclose anything, one keeps it private. One does not sit on another's bunk. Also, one does not turn on the forecastle light if that watch is asleep or make any unnecessary noise. One does not look into another's locker and let doors or locker doors slam. In plain words, one respects another's privacy. There is one watch of three men in one room, so one conducts oneself accordingly.

A ship has a motto: everything in its place and a place for everything. As a ship rolls and pitches everything must be secured so that it is not rolling or sliding around to injure someone or cause damage. That is always hard to impress on landlubbers on their first trip to sea. Everything that is done aboard ship in a certain way has a good reason for it being done that way through centuries of experience.

Seamen have a knack of recognizing one another ashore. The brotherhood of the sea actually exists but mostly in the hearts and minds of all who follow the sea. We will make extraordinary efforts to save or help other ships or seamen and history has recorded many such instances that have occurred over the centuries. Seafaring is a very hazardous industry, as one can read in the newspapers quite often about ships grounding, collisions, explosions or fires and the deaths and injuries of the personnel aboard, in spite of all the safety precautions that are taken. A great deal of the time, it is because of the human error or the sea itself, which is unpredictable.

Seamen drink a lot of coffee. There is always a pot brewing somewhere. There is a coffee pot on the bridge in the engine room and the ship's pantry.

When leaving port, the third mate goes to the bridge and tests the ship's whistle, running lights, steering gear, telephones, telegraph and the ship's radar. After undocking them, the work really commences, as the ship must prepare for sea. The mooring lines must be stored below on freighters. The cargo hatches are battened down the booms, lowered and secured, and the anchor's spill pipes cemented to keep water out of the chain lockers. All the work must be finished as we might have heavy seas outside of the harbor. The whole deck department continues working until the ship is secure for sea.

I cannot instill in you the sensation one has as the ship begins to pitch and roll gently on the first swells. With the sweet smells of fresh sea air, everyone aboard is happy to be away from the port and back on the sea. It is a feeling hard to describe to a landlubber.

The sea has such a strong attraction for men that they leave their wives and family to go to sea. Why is this so? What is this attraction? It is almost impossible to describe, unless one has been subject to it. Only seafarers know it. I myself had given up the sea but in the end, I could not resist the pull of the sea. A seaman ashore is like a fish out of the water, unable to exist outside of its environment.

It is not because it's a better life on board, as it is a Spartan life. We spend hours reading or playing cards or working on some hobby or sleeping or even washing or mending clothes. The steward puts out trays of cold cuts in the crew's mess room and in the saloon for the watches during the night as watch standers like to have a sandwich and a cup of coffee before going on watch. That has been a tradition for years.

Seamen have been discriminated against for centuries. In the United States, we were not included in the original Social Security bill; it was not until after the World War II that we were included. We were excluded from the forty-hour labor law. We were the only industry that had a standard fifty-six hour workweek without overtime and it was not until about 1950 that we were included. The politicians did not have any fear of us because we were such a small minority and could not cause them any problems at election time.

In spite of being on the same ship, there is a social structure. The master and deck officers consider themselves as premier officers of the ship. This goes back to centuries when there was only a master and deck officers. Then, with the advent of steam propulsion that brought engineers aboard, they were looked down upon as grease monkeys. The entire deck department did not consider them to be seamen.

This was a natural occurrence after centuries of sailing and it exists as an undercurrent even today. Deck officers tend to form friendships among themselves as you cannot associate with people to whom you have to give orders and the deck crew tends to do the same as they have more in common than they would with members of other departments. Everyone is friendly with one another but it seems that closer friendships seem to be made with members of their own departments.

I must mention an organization that has been wonderful to merchant seamen and provided us with vital entertainment. The American Merchant Marine Library Association furnishes books to seamen at no cost in every port in the United States. All one has to do is call them and they will bring a library down to the ship. I must also mention the Seamen's Church Institute, who has provided seamen with low-cost housing and food as they operate a large hotel in New York City and also supply spiritual counseling, if needed.

There are two types of shipping; one is coastwise shipping and the other intercoastal via the Panama Canal and foreign shipping. Most coastwise shipping consists of tankers running from oil refineries to various cities in the United States. There are also the container ships that ply the coastal trade.

A lot of seamen prefer the coastwise ships as some of them reside on one end or the other and can be relieved by other crew members so that they stay home with their families while the ship is in port.

Ship chandlers have existed for centuries as ships always

needed various supplies. At one time different people supplied certain goods, so a variety of tradesmen sold supplies to the ships until someone figured out how to supply all of the needed goods at one time and have only one delivery. Seamen soon learned to distrust ship's chandlers, as they would pass off substandard foods that could not be sold in the domestic market. To this day, ship's officers double-check all supplies received from the ship's chandlers. Some chandlers are worldwide as some ships have fast turnarounds and must be supplied within a limited time. Sometimes we do not have adequate time to inspect all the supplies and are stuck with poor quality goods.

Crew members are always trying to bring liquor aboard the ship as American maritime law prohibits liquor aboard and most ship captains strictly enforce the law of dry ships. Last but not the least, men are without sex for weeks. So, they look for it from prostitutes who frequent these places. I must point out that not all seamen drink or go with prostitutes. Some do not even go ashore but like to stay aboard in order to save their money. Another problem of going ashore in foreign ports is pilots, named after the pilot fish that are companions of sharks and live off the crumbs that sharks create while feeding. These pilots attach themselves to seamen and want to provide them with everything. They want to change your American money. They have small bills wrapped in one large roll. They make you believe they are giving you the right change and they scoot away and as you count your money, you find you have been taken for a ride.

These urchins have other tricks to play on you. If you have an expensive bracelet on your watch, they will snatch it off your wrist, and as the bracelet gives way, they disappear with it. A group of them will approach you and suddenly two or more will grab each arm and others will cut your wallet out of your pocket and dash away with it. It is almost impossible to catch them as they are so fast. Others will try and sell you their sisters or other women for sex. Boys also offer all kinds of souvenirs or any vice you can imagine, including any illegal drugs. It is amazing to find out about all the things in they are involved, as necessity breeds all these actions. But with the healthy economy of Europe you do not find much of this any longer there. But it is prevalent in other parts of the world like Central and South America, the Middle East, the Far East and Africa.

Chapter II
THE WAR YEARS

World War II took a tremendous toll on the lives and ships of the Merchant Marine. 2,710 liberty ships were built between 1941 and 1945. Of them, more than two hundred were lost during the war.

On just one convoy from Iceland to North Russia—Convoy PQ-17—thirty-five ships sailed but only twelve arrived, as this was the convoy that the British Navy abandoned and the German aircraft and submarines decimated. This convoy fought through a firestorm of bombs, torpedoes and sub-freezing water temperatures that would kill you in a matter of minutes. So if you did not have a chance to abandon the ship in a lifeboat or life raft, your chances of surviving were very slim.

Material losses by this convoy were 3,500 vehicles, 430 tanks, over 200 planes and 100,000 tons of other war cargo. Four of the ships lost were liberty ships.

The Germans destroyed 292 American ships during the year 1942 alone, and thirty-one ships were sunk with no survivors. 584 seamen were captured as prisoners of war. Forty-two seamen died while held prisoners of war by the Japanese, including the two that were executed by the Japanese on Wake Island. These prisoners were used to construct the bridge over the River Kwai. A movie was made publicizing their terrible ordeal. Of all the prisoners held there, the merchant seamen were the last to be repatriated out of Burma and brought to India. The army doctor who treated these men was so touched by their horrible condition that he cried. He also found some used army clothes for them as they had only rags to wear. It has to be said that the US Army was not very sympathetic towards these men who were brutalized by the Japanese—some for as long as three-and-a-half years.

Also, twenty seamen died while held as prisoners of the

Germans, but the Germans were not as brutal to merchant seamen as the Japanese.

We were in the war before our nation declared war as the German submarines and aircraft attacked and sunk and damaged twenty American ships while we were at peace with Germany. According to Maritime law, when you are separated from a ship due to injury, sickness or in wartime, your wages are terminated with the sinking of your ship. So, seamen who survived the sinking of their vessel did not receive any wages from that period on. After three-and-a-half years in a prisoner of war camp, the only wages they were paid is what they had earned up to the time the ship was lost. Everyone who survived any sinking or injury or sickness only received wages up to the time of the incident.

Seamen who were injured with war wounds or injuries were cared for. Those who were in need of longer treatment or medical custody were treated at the marine hospitals but if you later developed a secondary medical condition, you were out of luck as the marine hospital had a rule that a seaman applying for medical treatment had to have been employed as a seaman within sixty days prior to his application. After President Carter closed the marine hospitals, the seamen who were being treated since the war were turned out of the hospitals and had to turn to charities to get treatment, thanks to President Carter. No wonder he was so disliked by us seamen. He did more for foreigners than for American seamen.

On the other hand, I think fondly of the people of Nova Scotia who were wonderful to us while we were at anchor in Halifax awaiting for the convoy to sail. Some women came on board. I think it was some kind of seamen's society. I am not sure after all these years but I remember that they brought us woolen boots, socks, fur vests, woolen-knitted hats, scarves, sweaters, and mittens. Those gifts certainly kept us warm crossing that cold, windy, stormy, brutal north Atlantic. I will be eternally grateful to those wonderful women who gave us those wonderful warm clothes. We did not receive anything like that from our own people.

Likewise, we were treated magnificently by the people of Great Britain as they held merchant seamen in the highest degree.

As they are an island people, everything had to come by ship—food, all raw materials to manufacture goods—so that their lifeblood was their shipping. They realized the sacrifices we were making for them and treated us accordingly. Everything was rationed during the war and if we went to the ration board and told them that we were merchant seamen they asked us what we needed and then they would issue us coupons for shoes and clothes or work. I know personally, as I bought shoes and clothes myself because I was wearing out all of mine—some of the other crew members also did the same.

Another personal experience I had was while talking to a bobby, a British policeman, who was posted aboard our ship for our protection. I would occasionally give him sandwiches and coffee because everything was in short supply and rationed. So I happened to mention that I missed having milk, which we had not had for months. The next morning he came on board with a bottle of milk for me. I found out from another source that it was his ration for a whole week. I felt embarrassed by this kind act on his part.

By contrast to the way we were treated overseas, while we risked our lives carrying ammunition and everything that our troops needed to fight through submarine infested waters and axis war planes, there were two reporters accusing us of being overpaid and trying to sabotage our ships by carrying on board emery dust in our pockets to put in the ship's bearings, which were gross lies. Why these two reporters, Walter Winchell and Westbrook Pegler, dislike merchant seamen so much and tried to turn the public against us while we were dedicated to sailing our ships and delivering the supplies in spite of everything that the Germans and Japanese attacked us with, we don't know.

The seamen's union finally took them to court and won some big settlements against them and so shut down their propaganda against us.

In January 1942, the German U-boats appeared off our Atlantic coast and the sinking of our ships commenced. The ships were silhouetted against the shore lights. German submarine captains remarked that it was like shooting fish in a barrel as merchants ashore refused to dim their lights, saying that it would hurt their business. The commander of the Atlantic fleet, Admiral King, did not like the British system of convoys until President Roosevelt ordered him to implement it as, at that time, our maritime losses were staggering. Over one hundred tankers were sunk by the Germans trying to destroy our oil distributing system that would upset our war production.

We were the first industry to abolish discrimination in the maritime industry. President Franklin D. Roosevelt issued an executive order banning it. I have never experienced any problems aboard ships due to the mixed crew. In fact, in all my years of going to sea, I have found that seamen get along better than people ashore. You can't sleep and eat and work daily with these people and hold a grudge against them. We grew to respect one another, regardless of our race or color or religion. I guess we were further advanced than our counterparts who worked ashore.

In the maritime industry, there were always blacks working aboard some ships as some companies had what we used to call a checkerboard crew (black and whites). Blacks were only employed in the stewards department as cooks aboard and stewards utilities. No blacks were hired for the deck or engine departments. Why this pattern existed, I have no idea, as the first ship I ever sailed on before the war had a checkerboard crew.

At the beginning of the war, the safety equipment on ships was not in a good shape as steamship companies did not want to spend money on replacements or time repairing the equipment. It took the war to find out just how deficient ship's lifesaving equipment was.

Most ships had wooden lifeboats. When a tanker was torpedoed, most often the leaking cargo was set afire and burned up the wooden lifeboats and the crew that was in them also. The crew members swimming in the water died. What a horrible way to die! Can anyone imagine such a death?

The life jackets before the war were made of cork and seamen who were picked up out of the sea were found dead with broken necks. It seems that when they jumped overboard and hit the water, the water slammed the cork life jacket up under their chins, breaking their necks. They found a good substitute in kapok and replaced all of the lifejackets on all the ships, thus saving a few lives. All lifeboats from then on were manufactured with steel, eliminating that problem. On tankers, one of the lifeboats had to have a motor so that it could tow the other lifeboats out of danger.

Life rafts were also installed on ships to supplement the lifeboats in case they were damaged. There were two on the forward deck and two on the aft deck. The life rafts were credited with saving lives. Another thing which helped us were the little flashing red lights that were attached to our life jackets, enabling rescue ships to find us in the water at night. On a dark night it was almost impossible to see anyone in the water.

Later on, during the war, they came out with survival suits made out of rubber that enclosed your entire body except your face. You had to have your life jacket on under the suit to provide ample buoyancy.

Once we got to sea we slept in our clothes with our life jacket beside our bunk and our seamen passport and seamen's papers sewed up in canvas and attached to us with a small chain because, if the ship is torpedoed, sometimes the ship sinks in a matter of minutes and you would not have time to dress and it could cost you your life. Also, one never closed the door to the room. The key was always put on the door hook. If your ship was hit the ship would buckle and the doors would jam and you would be trapped in your room and thus would go down with the ship to a watery grave.

We experienced a loss of 820 ships and over 6,600 merchant seamen. Another discrimination against us was war risk insurance. The army, navy, coastguard and marines were given policies of ten thousand dollars but the US government felt that we were worthless and gave us policies of only five thousand dollars each.

President Franklin Roosevelt, when he signed the GI bill of rights on June 22, 1944 said, (and I quote) "I trust that the Congress will also provide similar opportunities for post-war education and unemployment insurance to the members of the merchant marine who have risked their lives time and time again during this war for the welfare of our country."

Five bills were considered during the 1940s and none were passed. I often wondered if our lives were more worthless than others' lives? No wonder we were so disillusioned and bitter towards our government. It was a hurt that was eating us alive inside. Forty-three years later, we were finally recognized as veterans, no thanks to the Veterans of Foreign Wars and the American Legion, who fought against every bill that was introduced in Congress to grant us veteran status. I don't think that the average serviceman thought that way because of all the contact that I had with them during the war when they would come aboard the ship for a meal or a cup of coffee and talk with us. I blame the upper officials of those organizations for treating us like the stepchild of the navy, as some of their members called themselves the bastards of the navy. The US Naval Armed Guard who sailed with us to man the guns aboard the ship—assisting, passing ammunition and being part of the gun crew—have wholeheartedly supported us in our efforts to become veterans. They also formed an organization, the US Naval Armed Guard of World War II, and invited us to join them.

Some of them had become very upset because the VFW has refused to let us join that body. They have also refused to join the VFW, saying that, If the guy next to me passing me the ammunition is refused, why should I join them?

An old adage says, "Better late than never," but late was the thing as it did not give us a chance to improve our education, buy a home, or get a loan for business because of our age. At the time of approval we were too old, so all that we received was the right to be buried with a flag in a national cemetery if one wanted to. In my opinion, it is a national disgrace that it took forty-three years to grant us what we should have had before the war ended.

Chapter III
MY FIRST LIBERTY SHIP

At the beginning of the war, I had sailed on a couple of old tankers. So I came to the conclusion that to ship on a brand new liberty ship, where everything would be new after all the old rusty buckets I had been on, would be a delightful change.

So I went down to Baltimore, Maryland. As I did not have too much money on hand, I thought that I could ship out fast as they were building ships in the new Bethlehem Steel Fairfield Yard. But I was in for a surprise when I went up to the NMU Union Hall. It was full of seamen. After registering I found that I had a high number and that it would be a while before I would have a low enough number to get a ship. The reason that there were so many men on the beach was that the German submarines had sunk so many ships after arriving off the East Coast of the United States that it had actually created a shortage of ships and a pool of unemployed seamen.

Those old tankers I had on which I had sailed had given me a couple of hair-raising experiences. We were chased a couple of times when nearing our coast by the German submarines trying to get in position to torpedo us. We zigzagged all over to escape them and succeeded in doing so as those ships had no life rafts and we had not been armed with guns yet. It sure was frightening.

The U-boat commanders attacked our ships and knew that we had nothing with which to defend ourselves and that they were attacking defenseless ships and seamen who were working at their trade by sailing ships and delivering cargo. We were facing a ferocious and merciless attack and no mercy was shown to the seamen killed. Those seamen struggled to survive on a flaming sea of burning oil. How many died a horrible death?

As I soon ran out of money, I decided I had to do something till I could shipped out. So I talked to the manager of the YMCA and was told that I could work cleaning up in the YMCA for my room rent. A friend of mine asked me to join him and he brought me with him to a soup kitchen. We just had to listen to the sermons to eat, but I soon got tired of that as I had no money to spend. So I went down to the unemployment bureau. After the interview, I was told that there was a job that would be ideal for me. It was a job at the Baltimore City Hospital being a waiter and cleaning up after the meals. It also provided room and board. I said, Great, and I took it until I was at the top of the shipping list. I threw my shipping card in on a new liberty ship getting ready to sail from the shipyard so I joined the ship in the Fairfield Yard. We spent about ten days storing the equipment and getting our quarters squared away.

We sailed on July 30 for Norfolk, Virginia. We went first into a degaussing dock to remove the residue magnetism that a ship develops during building. It has to be removed as it will attract mines and torpedoes. After it was finished, we shifted to a loading dock and commenced loading Army cargo. After finishing loading the hatches, we also took on a deck load of huge boxes, which contained crated up bombers and fighters. They were so large that they had to build a catwalk of wood so we could walk forward and aft with stairs to walk up to the top and across and down the stairs at the other end.

We then sailed for New York, picking up a Navy escort at Cape Henry, who escorted us all the way into New York harbor. We had to wait there for the convoy that was forming up. We left New York for Halifax, Nova Scotia on August 18, 1942. On the way up we collided with the Nantucket Lightship. It only caused slight damage to both of us. We arrived at Halifax on August 23, 1942 and anchored there, awaiting a convoy being made up to cross the North Atlantic.

We sailed from Halifax on August 30 and headed into the stormy North Atlantic Ocean and entered into the battle of the North Atlantic, stealthily followed by U-boats. There were attempts to attack us but they were forestalled by our escorts who continually depth charged them and beat them off of us. We succeeded in arriving at the British Isles and docked at the small city of Avonmouth on September 12, 1942. While in the process of docking, we struck an Australian freighter Waronga. The damage was minimal to both vessels. We suffered a slight dent in our bow. Avonmouth is small but the city of Bristol was only about five miles away. The damage by the German Air Force there was extensive.

From Bristol one could take a train to London. So one day when I was off, I took a train to London. After getting in at Victoria Station I went looking for a place to stay and someone told me that I could get a room at the Red Cross. It was in an old mansion so I booked a room at a very reasonable price. Then I went over to the Eagles Club which was the club formed by American pilots flying for the RAF. They welcomed us, as we were Americans. While talking to the bartender, he told me that the British Broadcasting Corporation was looking for a merchant seaman to make a broadcast to the United States. The bartender gave me the address and the manager's name. So I took a trip over there and had an interview. He chose me to make the broadcast, so I made a broadcast to the United States and a station in Providence, Rhode Island made a copy of the broadcast for me.

I went around London seeing all the sights: Westminster Abbey, Big Ben—the clock in the Parliament Building, the River Thames, St. Paul's Cathedral, Lord Nelson's statue, and Covent Garden. That also has a beautiful dance hall. They had afternoon dances that they called Tea Dances with an orchestra. They seemed to have more service people than civilians as most civilians were working in the war industries and would not have the time to attend dances.

One evening as I was coming out of the subway I found that the city of London was undergoing an air raid. I immediately dove back down into the subway and stayed there until it was over. I soon learned how to move about in a blackout as everything was blacked out in Great Britain during the war, including buses, trains and taxis. After a few days, I had to return to the ship so I went to Victoria Station and caught a train back to Bristol and then a bus to Avonmouth.

The ship was unloaded by black army troops. After we were completely unloaded there, we sailed over to Newport. There they installed additional twenty milliliter guns and also built a galley and living quarters in the 'tween decks in the number five hold. They also began to load the ship again. We also took on thirty-one US Army soldiers and twenty-five British sailors along with a deck load of two LCI which was lashed down on the forward deck as we had a fifty-ton boom on the foredeck that could be used to lift up and discharge the LCIs.

On October 20, 1942 we shifted to Swansea to take on fuel and water. On October 21, we sailed up to the Clyde River and anchored, awaiting for the convoy to form. On October 23, the convoy sailed for destination unknown. Some submarines were sighted but were driven off by the navy escorts. We were finally told that we were part of the invasion group going to invade North Africa.

On November 6, we met up with the convoy from the United States off the coast of Spain at Gibraltar. What a sight that was! Hundreds of ships coming together with troop ships, freighters and tankers.

The whole huge convoy entered the Mediterranean Sea. Our ship proceeded past the city of Oran to Arzew. We anchored because of the shellfire from the French Foreign Legion Fort. We finally received orders to dock. We went into the harbor and tied up to the dock. We were the first ship to dock in North Africa. It was quite hair-raising for a while as we could hear the ricocheting bullets. Before coming into the dock, we unloaded the LCI into the water with the fifty-ton boom and the British sailors ran them into the harbor. After docking, we found out that the army troops that we had carried down here were supposed to unload the ship. Had we known this we could have given them some training on the way down to the Mediterranean. While we lay at anchor, we got the ship ready by raising the booms and positioned them for discharging cargo. That is when we found out that these soldiers had not had any training on how to unload a ship. When their first load of 500 lb bombs was slammed against the side of the ship, we—the crew—took over the operation of the cargo winches. I took over number four hatch winches as I could look right down into the hold from where I was running the winches. I directed what to send up next and how to connect the cargo wires and nets. I worked seventy-two hours without rest. The stewards department brought us coffee and sandwiches to keep us going. I was relieved once so I could get some sleep. When I woke up I went out and worked until we finished discharging the ship. We then went out and anchored in the harbor to wait for a convoy. As we were securing the ship for sea, we heard somebody shouting. We looked over the side of the ship and there, along the side of the ship, was one of the LCI that we had brought with us with some of the army guys and some British sailors operating the landing craft and they had a great big hogshead of wine. It must have been at least 500 gallons, if not more. They said, "We pushed this off of the dock where it was waiting shipment to France." They said, "You guys were so good to us we wanted to do something for you so we rigged the booms and hauled it aboard and stowed it in number three hatch 'tween deck." We had pitchers of wine on all the tables at meal times until the captain got so drunk one day and started giving all sorts of crazy orders so the second mate took it upon himself and went down in the hold and chopped a hole in the bottom of the wine barrel and let it all run out into the permanent ballast and that was the end of the wine episode. While we were in the port of Arzew the third assistant engineer and a wiper decided to go over to the city of Oran and see the sights. Well, they didn't realize that there was intense fighting going on. The last I saw of them they were walking up the road from the dock. We never found out what happened to them. The ship never got any report that they might have gotten killed as the area they passed through was very dangerous.

I have wondered till this day if they ever reached Oran without being killed. Before leaving, I had talked one of the British Navy sailors into selling me his navy coat, because I knew that I needed something warmer in the North Atlantic. This was a great coat made out of wool with a hood and wooden toggles and loops instead on buttons that prevented the wind from opening up your coat. I had that coat for years after the war. It was the warmest coat that I have ever had.

While we were heading for Gibraltar, we encountered German

planes four times in one day, but they had sunk two ships in a convoy behind us. Also, our escorts sunk a submarine very close to us. We were lucky that day.

After arriving at Gibraltar, we waited there for the formation of another convoy going to Great Britain. We anchored at Gibraltar and put ashore the rest of the British sailors. After leaving Gibraltar, the convoy was attacked again by submarines and they had been stalking us. On November 20, two of our British escorts attacked a submarine from about 2 P.M. to sundown, dropping depth charges, and destroyed one.

We passed to the west and north of Ireland and then proceeded to the port of Liverpool. After passing the Isle of Man we docked in Liverpool on November 24.

Liverpool is one of the largest ports in Great Britain, with seven miles of docks which were extensively damaged by the German Air Force.

While entering the harbor, we could see all the ships that were sunk in the Mersey River and in the harbor itself. There are two ports there. Liverpool, and across the Mersey River lies The City of Birkenhead. Some of the crew and Navy gun crew went across the river to Birkenhead via the two modes of transportation. One was the ferry and the other was the tunnel, which burrowed under the Mersey River. I also made another trip to London as there was so much to see there.

London was originally a group of small cities that grew together over the centuries. Westminster was where most of the government was centered and the king resided there in ancient times. There were so many historical buildings and sights to see, like Hyde Park, where anyone could stand on a box or platform and talk about any subject you wanted to. Of course, the biggest attraction for the crew was girls. They were plentiful because of the shortage of men as the British Armed Forces were fighting all over the world.

The Americans were very popular with the British women. One heard remarks about the Yanks that they were overpaid, oversexed and over here. I believed it was because Americans had more money and could afford to spend on them. The crew didn't have much competition because most of the American troops and

Air Force were stationed more in the Central and Southeastern England. There were very few stationed on the west coast of Great Britain. The Germans destroyed a lot of the English ports by trying to demolish the cargo handling facilities of Britain as its life depended on shipping. If they succeeded in destroying the ports and merchant ships, they could starve Great Britain and destroy her morale and cause her to surrender. In the meantime, our ship was being loaded. In order to understand what happened on our voyage, I shall explain the cargo setup of a liberty ship. It has five holds or hatches. Starting from just aft of the bow is #1 hold; aft of that is #2 hold and then #3 hold, which ends at the amidship house where most of the crew and officers live and also contains the mess rooms, galley and stewards stores. The #4 hold is aft of the amidship house and a part of the 'tween decks protrudes under the house. The reason I am explaining this is because when the ship was loaded this space was full of ammunition. #1 hold was filled with army cans of gasoline; #2-3-4-5 were loaded with ammunition from thirty caliber bullets, artillery shells of all calibers, 500 lbs bombs and depth charges. We were a floating armory.

On December 16, 1942 we embarked forty-seven British soldiers and on December 18 we sailed from Liverpool to an anchorage just outside of the mouth of the Mersey River and dropped anchor to wait for a convoy on December 19. We sailed at 9 P.M. heading north. On December 20, we arrived at the River Clyde, anchored at Loch Ewe and again waited for the convoy to form. All this time the weather was cold and foggy and miserable and I was so happy that I had that British navy coat which kept me warm. We sailed on December 24 at 5 P.M. That was Christmas Eve and I can tell you, it was not a very happy crew as everyone was walking around with long and sad faces. On Christmas, we had an excellent dinner but everyone's thoughts were of family and home. I don't think many of the British soldiers enjoyed Christmas dinner because most of them were so seasick. I felt sorry for them but there is not much you can do for seasickness. We were really heavily loaded on this trip as we were also carrying four tanks on our fore deck. We had to keep checking the lashings on them because the ship was rolling and pitching heavily due to stormy weather.

On January 5, we entered the Mediterranean, passing by Gibraltar. We heard planes and anti-aircraft fire from the Rock of Gibraltar. The Mediterranean was very rough at this time. On January 6, 1943, we saw our escorts depth charging a submarine. Our convoy was turned around. Due to aircraft, we turned around and passed by Oran, North Africa.

On January 7, we passed by Algiers at about 8 A.M. and could see a lot of planes over the city—bombers and fighters. We continued heading east towards Phillipville, our destination, which was very close to the front lines.

At about noon on January 7, our escorts suddenly opened fire and as we looked about, we saw that they were firing on an observing German plane that was circling the convoy above the range of the guns. Everybody was saying we were going to get it tonight when dusk fell. All hell broke loose. Every ship opened fire *JU-88* upon the dive-bombers that were attacking us from above and ahead of us. While we were engaged in firing at them, we didn't notice the *Heinkle 111*'s coming in at mast height from our port side.

When the attack started, I was on lookout on the bow of the ship. Evidently, the phone of the three-and-a-half inch forward gun went out of order. So I was asked to go to the bridge and bring a replacement. On my way back up to the bow I began to see these red dots flashing by the front of me. It took a few seconds to penetrate my mind that these were bullets flashing by. I made a quick dive to the deck beside one of the hatches. The German planes were strafing the ships while attacking us.

We were suddenly hit with a bomb in number one hold but there was no explosion. While I was still on lookout, I watched a ship get hit just ahead of us but in the next column, there was a tremendous explosion and the ship disintegrated in one loud roar. I could hear men screaming in the water. I shall carry that sound with me until my dying day. It was horrible and we felt so horrified as we could do nothing for them as ships were forbidden to stop while underway in a convoy.

When we were hit in number one hold, my watch partner Ted Rosata had a three-inch shell in his hands ready to insert it into the breech on the gun. When the ship was struck he was knocked down but had enough presence of mind to get up and throw the shell overboard as the fuse had been struck. If it had gone off it would have killed the whole gun crew. Another plane dropped a bomb and just missed us. It exploded just off our starboard bow. While heading back to amidship, I saw a plane hit a ship just astern of us on the port side and it disappeared in a great blast. His flight took him across our stern and our gunners poured fire into him. I could see the shells striking him as he crashed into the sea. During the attack our ship shot down five German planes in over seventy minutes. I then went up on the ship's bridge as it was my turn to steer the ship. While I was steering, there was another near miss by a bomb that exploded alongside the bridge. The concussion heeled the ship over and threw water over the flying bridge. It also knocked the ship's compass down to the bottom of the binnacle and I had to steer the ship by following the ship just ahead of us.

If that bomb had gone off in number one hold, we would have disappeared like the other ships which had been hit.

The military that planned the arrangement of the convoy stationed the tankers and ammunition carrying ships in the center of the convoy. As if the Germans didn't know that. They came directly after our ship in the beginning of the air attack. I think that what saved the rest of the convoy were the two British ships which were called ack-ack ships. They were converted merchant ships that had nothing but anti-aircraft guns and they could pour out a tremendous amount of anti-aircraft fire and finally drove off the attacking planes.

In the meanwhile, we were heading for port Phillipville. As we were sinking by the head, the convoy commander contacted us and inquired if we could possibly make port. The Captain replied, "We will beach her if we have to as we want to deliver our cargo." We finally made port at 8:00 A.M. the next day and docked. We were very close to the front as we could hear the artillery and close to us the LCT were constantly discharging tanks and equipment and troops. They would head for the front as soon as they were discharged.

A crew of Algerians started discharging our cargo. As there were constant air raids the longshoremen would frantically abandon the ship by any means and fly up the dock as if the devil himself was chasing them. We in the meanwhile were painting the ship's hull.

The Army forbade us to fire our guns as they said that would target us so we took no steps to defend ourselves.

When enough gasoline cans were discharged to expose the bomb, a squad of British demolishing experts came aboard to defuse the bomb. They did so and we were told that they could find nothing wrong with the bomb's fuse and could not understand why it did not go off. It was found lying up against the bulkhead of the ammunition locker. We kept the defused bomb aboard the ship and stowed it back aft just outside of the US Naval Armed Guard after quarters, where we had workbench for the deck department. If that bomb had gone off, I would not be here today writing this story. On the way back, the gun crew and the deck gang scraped out the powder inside the shell of the bomb. Youth will do dangerous things without thinking. I, too, cut a piece of that bomb off and kept it for years. I misplaced it one time while moving. I had kept it as a reminder of my mortality.

At 5:00 P.M. on January 17, 1943, after being discharged, we left the dock and shifted to an anchorage in the bay to wait for a convoy.

We sailed from anchorage at 2:00 A.M. on January 18, 1943. That evening, near Cape Carbon, we were again attacked by German planes in a heavy air raid between 4:00 and 5:00 P.M. and then attacked again at about 8:00 P.M. that same evening.

On January 19, 1943, we were again heavily attacked by planes at about 10:00 P.M.

We arrived at Gibraltar on January 23 at 10:00 A.M. and entered the Harbor of Gibraltar. In order to have a patch installed over the hole of number one hatch on the port side, we at first thought that they were going to weld a steel patch over the hole but decided to put a temporary patch—one of cement—and do the repairs in England.

After they completed installing the cement patch, we were sent out to anchor just outside the harbor but it was not very pleasant for us as all night long the British had patrol boats circling the ships at anchor and dropping depth charges as there were frog men swimming from a German ship that was partially sunk in Spanish waters. The Germans were using it as a station to attack our ships at anchor. They would swim across Gibraltar Bay and attach mines to the hulls and sink ships. The British Navy counter-attacked by dropping depth charges that would kill the swimmers in the water.

As we had shore leave in Gibraltar, I explored around by wandering the streets for sightseeing. While walking down a side street I spotted a sign that said purveyor of wines and spirits so I said to myself, I have nothing to lose by going in and finding out if I could buy some scotch whiskey, as during the war it was almost impossible to obtain scotch whiskey.

So I went in and started talking to the proprietor. I finally sweet-talked him into selling me two bottles of scotch. He then told me he would sell me some but on the condition that I would not tell anyone where I purchased it. I agreed and off I went with the two bottles of scotch. As it was pretty cool, I had my overcoat on and the bottles fitted nicely in my overcoat, one in each side pocket.

Everyone on the ship tried to get me to reveal where I obtained the whiskey but I would not reveal my source. So every day I went ashore and visited my new friend at the spirit shop and purchased two more bottles. As we were at anchor and in ballast, our only means of boarding the ship was climbing up a pilot ladder. All my shipmates carefully watched my progress up the ladder as they knew I had the whiskey in my overcoat pockets. I think they were more worried about the whiskey than my safety.

On February 7, 1943 at about 6:00 P.M., we sailed out through the mine nets at Gibraltar and started forming a convoy. During the night, a submarine torpedoed the Commodore of the convoy. His ship was loaded with iron ore and sank very fast. Our escort, trying to find the submarines, fired so many flares that the sky was lit up like day. The gun crew stood by for the rest of the night.

On February 15, 1943, early in the morning, we approached the minefields of the St. George's Channel that had been closed with mines for over two years. The British decided to open it up to save mileage from going around the west side of Ireland. The minefields were over fifty miles long and we passed into the Irish Sea.

The sea was very rough. It was raining and cold. It was just miserable weather.

On February 16, 1943, we anchored at the mouth of the Mersey River. While we were in Phillipville, everyone was buying tangerines and oranges. They were so cheap as the farmers could not ship them to France—their normal market—due to the war. There was a glut on the market and we took advantage of it and purchased a large amount to eat. While passing through the locks at the port of Liverpool, people were standing on the breakwaters watching the ships entering the locks. They noticed that some of the crew members were eating citrus fruit and asked if we would give them some, so we started throwing some oranges and tangerines to them. They got very excited to receive citrus fruit as they had not eaten any since the war had started as the refrigerated ships had been sunk by U-boats. Whatever ships were left could not be spared to carry fruit as they were needed to carry more essential cargo for the prosecution of the war. The German submarines had decimated the British Merchant Marine.

On February 21, 1943, we sailed from Liverpool and were sailing down the Mersey River to the Irish Sea. As we continued to have engine trouble we were ordered back to Liverpool for repairs. We had been damaged by the bombs from air attacks that had put our engine shaft out of line.

At 6:30 P.M. we turned around and headed back to Liverpool and docked again for engine repairs. Repairs were completed on March 3, 1943 and once more we sailed from Liverpool and joined a convoy heading for the USA. The weather was bad, with heavy seas, wind with snow. We were in ballast so we were bouncing around quite a bit.

As I was on the four-to-eight watch, after getting off watch at 8:00 A.M. I went to the mess room and ate breakfast. After breakfast I thought I would take a look outside and opened the portside watertight door and stepped outside into the outside passageway. There was an accumulation of snow on the deck. I then noticed a crack through the snow as it ran to the edge of the deck plate. I took a glance over the ship's side and I saw that the crack ran down the ship's hull. I notified the ship's chief mate and all of the ship's officers went out to inspect the crack. They reported this to the convoy commodore.

As we approached Newfoundland, we were detached from the convoy with a destroyer for protection and entered the Port of St. Johns Newfoundland for repairs.

We tied up alongside a British ship while we were having that crack welded as the ship could have split into two. It was quite a repair job as the refrigerators were in the way.

We soon discovered the British ship had a full load of Queen Ann Scotch aboard and some of it soon found its way aboard our ship. Another great treat was obtaining fresh stores as we had been months without fresh fruits, vegetables and milk.

The steward had ordered 125 gallons of fresh milk at breakfast. We were told that the milk was all gone. It seems that the gun crew had gotten into the refrigerators that night and drank all of the milk. That created a little dissension among us. That was the first time because we all got along quite well during the entire time we were aboard this ship.

We went ashore here in St. Johns but it was cold as the main streets were parallel to the slope of the hill. It was fine as long as we walked along the main streets but when we started to walk down the hill, that was trouble as we started to slide and slip. We had no choice in the matter as the launch was downhill on the waterfront. The people in St. Johns were very friendly towards us and everybody enjoyed their stay there.

On March 25, 1942, the repairs were completed and we sailed for Halifax, Nova Scotia under escort of the Canadian Navy. The weather was still very cold.

On March 28, we arrived at Halifax and anchored outside of the submarine nets until the morning of March 29, 1943, when we entered the harbor passing through the minefields.

As we had a big snowfall the previous night and had quite a bit of snow on the main deck, the navy gun crew had a snow fight like a bunch of kids.

On March 31, 1943, we sailed from Halifax at 2:00 P.M. and formed a convoy heading for New York. We were the commodore ship on the way to New York. We ran aground on Cape Ann. The captain tried to work the ship off of the Cape but was not successful. Then a destroyer that was escorting us fired a line across our stern and we passed our hawsers to him. Even with our engines going full astern and the destroyer pulling us, the operation was not successful. We then waited for high tide and we floated off of Cape Ann. Boy, we really razzed the commodore and the ship's officers for such poor navigation as we were getting anxious to get back home after all this time.

We passed through the Cape Cod Canal and on April 3, 1943, we anchored at New York Harbor.

The Navy removed the Armed Guard Crew from the ship and, after clearing US Customs and Immigration, we hove up anchor and proceeded to the Brooklyn Shipyard and tied up. We were free to go. After getting an advance on my wages as the ship was not going to be paid off for a few days, I headed for my brother's apartment. We had to stay in New York until payday and that was the end of my voyage aboard the SS *William Wirt*.

We were to experience culture shock after arriving in the United States after being away so long. When we had left the States, all the things we now encountered were not in place, such as rationing, and New York City was afloat with uniforms. We had never seen uniforms of waves, WAC, lady marines, merchant marine officers and maritime school uniforms, as the government had opened up these schools and opened up the armed forces to women. We had become accustomed to the British uniforms of the Ats, Wrens, WRAF and the women land army uniforms as they were part of the scenery when we had arrived in Great Britain.

But to see all these new uniforms in the United States was quite a shock. Also, merchant seamen were only allowed so much leave time after a voyage and if you did not return to sea after your leave expired, you were subject to being drafted. I think I was allowed ninety days after this last voyage.

We had to take our leave certificate to the ration board and they gave us ration coupons according to the shore leave time we were allowed.

Transportation was one of our biggest problems as trying to find a seat on a train was almost impossible. I don't remember how many times I had to stand in the back of a coach from NY to Providence and vice versa. The coaches were jammed with service men traveling on leave or between posts.

Also, a lot of women were traveling to join their husbands wherever they were stationed to spend as much time with them as they could. In many cases that was the last time they saw them. Of course, girlfriends and parents also did the same.

Traveling in wartime was frantic, uncomfortable, extremely crowded, frustrating and dirty. But during this period we all let our emotions show more than we would have in normal times. It was a time of shortages, rationing, long lines to purchase even ration goods, and it was a very frustrating time to live, especially for parents, wives, families, friends and girlfriends praying and hoping they would not be receiving telegrams.

I think that one of the institutions most Americans enjoyed in the British Isles was the *pub*. It was completely different from any bar and saloon that we had in the United States.

It was a gathering place for families and friends as most of the pubs had cubicles that a family could occupy. Many friendships and romances were started here and an unknown number of marriages occurred by the romances started in the pubs. A lot of families welcomed us into their groups.

I also got acquainted with the manager of a pub in a small hotel in Liverpool. As we talked one evening, he told me he was quite fond of American tobacco and hinted that if he could obtain some that he could always have some scotch whiskey available for me. As I did not smoke, it was no problem for me to obtain my tobacco ration in pipe tobacco. It was certainly a fine friendship we worked out together.

My next wartime voyage was also on a liberty ship from New York to Liverpool, England. We encountered some new tactics from the German submarines as our anti-submarine measures became more sophisticated and new methods of finding and attacking them from the coast drove them farther out into the North Atlantic. Also, they were driven away from the shores from Great Britain. So, that left an area in the North Atlantic that could not be covered. The German Naval High Command devised new tactics with the Wolf Pack that could operate past the range of our planes from the United States, Iceland and Great Britain. So, the German Navy stationed picket submarines across the Atlantic intersecting our convoy routes. After a picket submarine spotted a convoy, it would shadow the convoy until it figured out the convoy's course and speed. They would then surface at night and relay the course and speed to German Naval Headquarters, who would then order the U-boats to assemble at specific positions along the convoy's route. After assembling, they would attack the convoy from several different points with great success. They drove the escorts crazy as they could not cover and attack every submarine.

We were fortunately placed in this trip as we were stationed in the center of the convoy and the ships being sunk were on the outer fringe of the convoy. The crew was certainly relieved to arrive at the mouth of the Mersey River and sail up to Liverpool and dock.

What a surprise I had! The port had been heavily damaged since my last trip there. Evidently, they had some heavy air attacks by the German Air Force because where I remember some docks had stood now there was nothing but a gaping hole.

I did not go up to London on this trip as I had too many duties to catch up with. After discharging all of our cargo we formed into a convoy and headed back to the States for another load.

This next voyage turned out to be an exciting one. As all merchant ships were overloaded by two feet, as the United States Government had suspended all regulations during the war, all ships were placed in a dangerous condition as we had so much less buoyancy than we should have according to load line laws.

My ship took on a load of coal in Norfolk, Virginia and we joined a convoy at the entrance to Chesapeake Bay. We started our voyage across the Atlantic and we had the misfortune to run into a hurricane.

Our lifeboats were swung out as all ships had them swung out in order to lower them swiftly because if you were torpedoed it was essential to lower the lifeboats swiftly to abandon the ship before you were carried down with it. In order to keep the lifeboats from swinging wildly, we had what was called a pudding spar. It had bumpers on them and were set in cradles that were welded onto the lifeboat *Davids* and a steel wire strap that was passed around the outside of the boat and secured on the boat deck with a quick release hook.

During this raging hurricane, the ship was swamped by monstrous waves that swept all sorts of equipment overboard. Our gangway was swept overboard and it had been well secured with the platform that is attached to the ship's hull.

A great wave came aboard and lifted the lifeboat. It lay in the cable. The Chief Mate called me to see what I could do to save the lifeboat. I called some of the deck gang who were off watch and we took some lines and wire cable with us. As night had fallen, we could not use lights as ships were forbidden to show any light at sea because a submarine could spot it.

It is very difficult to work in the dark. I got up into the lifeboat with some line and I passed them around the outside of the boat and handed the ends back to my helpers on the boat deck. I helped them fasten it. Just as I got out of the boat, another huge wave came on board and carried the lifeboat away. My helpers were yelling, "The bosun was carried overboard." I said, "No, I haven't. Here I am." That was the second time I escaped death during the war.

The convoy finally ran out of the hurricane. It had caused a lot of damage but at least we were still afloat, to the great relief of everyone on board.

As we approached the Italian Coast, we received a message from the convoy Commodore to detach ourselves from the convoy and anchor off the coast of Sicily. We anchored right under the shadow of Mount Vesuvius, which had a red glow all the time we were anchored there. Everyone was hoping she wouldn't blow while we were anchored here. And fortunately she stayed dormant during our stay. We had all kinds of visitors while at anchor. The Sicilians would come out to the ship in boats trying to sell things and buy clothes. I sold my suit and got a good price for it. We stayed at anchor for almost a month and we were all puzzled as to the reason why we stayed there so long. We were at war and ships were badly needed.

We finally got orders to proceed to Bari, Italy on the way up the Adriatic Sea. We were buzzed by our *B-17 Bombers*, which were stationed at Forgia, where the Army Air force had a large base. When we arrived at Bari, we knew the reason why we had been at anchor for so long. It seems that they had one of the war's worst catastrophes at Bari, Italy. On December 2, 1943, the harbor of Bari was brightly lit and packed with shipping ships loaded with troops and ammunition when a flight of 105 *JU-88s* attacked the Port of Bari, Italy. Somehow, the planes were never picked up by the radar so no air raid alarm went off. The German Air Force had a field day as the port was lit up like a day.

I had heard that there were about 5,000 army troops aboard some ships at anchor in Bari Harbor, as they had not been disembarked after arrival, a great mistake that the US Army did not repeat again.

The German air attack was a terrible maelstrom of bombs exploding, ships sinking and exploding in a great blast, killing everyone aboard them. The air was full of screams of the wounded and bodies floating in the harbor. Of the twenty-four ships in the harbor at the time of the raid, seventeen were destroyed. Of the seventeen ships, six were American ships. The only survivors were some of the ship's crew who were ashore during the attack. Of the American seamen aboard those ships, fifty-eight bodies were recovered with one hundred and fifty missing. The fifty-eight bodies were buried in the Military Cemetery there.

Why was a censure placed on this event? This is not mentioned in the war histories. The numbers of the army killed have never been revealed to this day but among seamen we knew. As we are a fluid membership, when we meet one another in different ports the story passes on from one to another. Bari must have been a lovely city before the war as it still had nice large boulevards with mosaic sidewalks. There were also lots of artistic people left in the city. I purchased a lot of cameos to bring back. You could see a lot of tragedies here but that must have happened all over Europe during the war. I witnessed women whose husbands had either been killed or were prisoners of war; who had children and no income due to the missing husbands and had to do anything they could to support themselves. The children went as far as selling their mother's bodies for money. We witnessed so much misery that we became immune to the sight of it.

After discharging part of the cargo of coal, we sailed up the coast to the port on Ancona, which was interesting as it had an old port and a new model that was supposed to be a showplace for the Italian Fascist Government. It was composed of all new homes with a shopping center in the middle of it. It was quite interesting, but it was only a showpiece.

After discharging all our cargo, we were sent to North Africa to load army cargo to bring it back to Italy. We also brought back some Italian prisoners of war. One of the prisoners started talking to me while they were getting some exercise on the deck. He could speak pretty good English. He told me he had lived in the States for a while in Chicago. He mentioned that he was a cook, so I talked him into cooking for us. Our ship's cooks were terrible and I was dying to eat some Italian cooking as I had grown very fond of it from visiting my Italian friends at home. Italian mothers always insisted on my eating even if I was not hungry. The prisoner cooked for us until we reached Italy. There they were removed from the ship. What a loss that was! From Italy, we returned to the States.

I remember a voyage during the war that really surprised me. It was actually not the voyage but what we carried. We sailed out of New York through the Panama Canal and stopped in all the ports along the west coast of South America and what did we discharge? Automobiles, washers, tires, radios. All of the goods we could not purchase in the States because of rationing. I had entertained thoughts about buying some automobile tires for my 1939 Olds and bringing the tires home. I was soon cured of the notion as I found out that it was against the law even though the tires were manufactured in the States. I could not re-enter them into the States. What a disappointment!

On the return trip, we loaded copper ingots in Chile and stopped in Ecuador for balsa wood. While loading, some Indians came alongside the ship in dugout canoes selling bananas. I bought a whole stalk of them. Those were the largest bananas I had ever seen, so I hung them in our forecastle—which is what we call our room. That name goes back to the old sailing ship days, when our quarters were in the forepart of the ships.

After I had been pulling off bananas from the stalk and eating them, one night I was lying in my bunk reading and I happened to glance at the overhead (what landlubbers would call a ceiling). There was a tarantula spider. He must have been at least six inches across. I soon sent him to a hasty end but we kept pulling bananas off of the stalk and eating them. A couple of nights later, I found another one, not as large. I dispatched him shortly after seeing him or her. I didn't pause to investigate.

Another day, as I was reaching for a banana, I saw one on the stalk and dispatched it. My roommates and watch partners were really upset. They said, "If you find another, we're not sleeping in here any more. We will sleep up on the fantail deck." But I had read that tarantulas are not very aggressive as long as you don't squeeze them.

I also made some trips in the Pacific. There was a shortage of seamen on the west coast, so the shipping administration hired us in New York and shipped us out to San Francisco by rail. We were exhausted by the time we got there. Trying to sleep on seats for four nights was not very pleasant and we had to change trains in Chicago.

The ship we joined was a fast American Export Lines ship that could do twenty-two knots. It was a combination troop and cargo ship. We sailed along the ship, zigzagging constantly so that we would not be torpedoed. We loaded on board a regiment of black troops and some army cargo. Some of it was beer but the crew was forbidden to touch the beer. We would not have touched it anyway because it had Atabrine in it. Everyone in the Army had to take it regularly and they all had a nice yellow complexion.

The first port we arrived at in New Guinea was Milne Bay, where we discharged some cargo. We were also able to see a USO show. We learned that they had just hung thirteen GIs for raping an army nurse. It was a quick trial and hanging.

There was a lovely natural pool where a river flowed over a cliff. It was a waterfall. We were told about it by the troops there, so some of the crew, including myself, went out to it and swam ala natural as nobody had swimming trunks. We had a great time in that terrible hot climate. It was so refreshing. We then proceeded up to Hollandia where there was a large army hospital. The black troops disembarked and the cargo was being discharged. We could see the troops drinking the beer on the beach. How they could drink that hot beer puzzled all of us on board, as we had transited the whole South Pacific and that beer had been exposed to that heat all that time. I don't know what the temperature of it was but it had to be very hot. It must have tasted good to them.

While we were in Hollandia, some army guys pointed out a large house up on a hill and told us that was General MacArthur's mansion and he had the army build it for him. He was not very popular with the army enlisted men. They were living in the mud and tents and he was living in a great big house.

The next day, we saw these men marching up the dock. It was the same troops we had just disembarked the day before. Some general did not want them there and shipped them back on board. We sailed up to the Island of Biak that had just been captured and discharged our troops again.

While we were there, a couple of us went up to a ridge where the Japanese had made their last stand. We could still see skeletons and all sorts of ammunition lying around. We picked some up and I still have some at home.

The stench up there from decaying corpses of Japanese soldiers was nauseating. After discharging all our cargo, we proceeded back to Hollandia to pick up guys who had been wounded in battle, had been treated and healed at the hospital and were now being returned to their regiment. While underway, I got friends with a guy that came from Boston. Just before arriving at his disembarking port, he called me aside and asked me if I would do him a favor. I told him, it depends on what the favor was. He then showed me a bag full of black pearls that he wore around his neck and asked me if I would take them to his wife in Boston. I told him I would like to, but I feared being caught with them by the US Customs. I always regretted not doing it for him. For all I know he might not have lived as he was an infantryman. I always hoped that he survived the war. I still think of him. He was not the only one who had taken things off dead Japanese soldiers. Others had gold teeth and gold fillings taken out of the mouths of Japanese.

After disembarking our troops, we returned to Hollandia and took on some more badly wounded soldiers who were being returned to the States for further treatment. We were also bringing back seven pregnant nurses. There were rumors that some nurses made a fortune servicing the army. Maybe that is how some of them got pregnant?

The master sergeant of the medical detachment got to be good friends as he was from Providence, Rhode Island so we would get together in the evening and have a few drinks, medical alcohol, either with pineapple, grapefruit, or tomato juice.

One day, the Chief Mate said, "I have a special job for you," and took me down in a lower passageway. It seemed somebody had removed a bolt in bulkhead—or wall, as you landlubbers would say. With the bolt removed, one could see into the nurses' room. So I looked in the storeroom and found the right bolt, went and screwed it in and then went into the nurses' room and hammered it over so that it could not be removed.

The South Pacific was a hot humid place and the islands were full of unknown tropical diseases, as much as all kinds of poisonous snakes and insects that most Americans had never encountered before. I bet that the troops must have shouted with great joy when they found that they were leaving their tropical paradises.

On the way back to San Francisco we ran out of food stores. Either the steward had not ordered enough before we left San

Francisco or he fed more people than he expected, so we were to get a big treat eating army rations. After eating them for a few days, I came to the conclusion that it was a great joy not to be in the army and to have to eat that food. In fact, it was a great pleasure to avoid it.

After arriving at San Francisco, I decided that I had enough of the South Pacific and decided to return to the East Coast. A friend who shipped out with me from New York and was of the same opinion as I decided to travel with me.

We found out that we could not get passage on a train until the next day, so we rented a hotel together for the night. After leaving our sea bags in the room, we decided to go for our little libation. As I had not had a drink of scotch since the beginning of the trip, after a few hours and a fair amount of scotch I thought I might as well go back to the hotel and rest up for the long journey by train to the East Coast. My friend decided to move around to see if he could find some female companionship. So off I went to the hotel room and promptly fell asleep. The next thing I remember is being shaken by my friend saying, "Jerry! Jerry! Get up! We have to leave right away." I looked at my watch and saw that we had plenty of time to catch the train. I said to him, "What's the big hurry?" He then told me the reason why.

It seems he had picked up this young woman in a nightclub and talked her into going to a hotel room with him for the night. During the night of romance, he found out that the girl was a virgin and that her father was the owner of the club. California had at that time a statutory rape law, which would put him in the big house for twenty years. You can imagine how fast we moved after he told me he couldn't get out of California soon enough.

He was lucky, as we caught the next train heading for Chicago, but it was a miserable trip as we had no seats. We had to stand or sit on the floor. I parked myself in the space after the last seat and the wall. I even slept there. Four days later, we were at Chicago and changed trains. He transferred to one going to New York and I transferred to one going to Boston. I was fortunate to have a seat all the way to Boston.

That was the last time I saw my friend, as our paths have never crossed again. The next ship I shipped on was loading a cargo of wheat. After the completion of loading, we shifted out to Anchorage in New York Harbor to wait for the formation of a convoy. While at anchor, another ship under was underway to anchor. The pilot must have misjudged his distance and speed and collided with us, hitting us in number two hold and punching a hole in us. The wheat had to be discharged from number two hold as it was all wet.

After it was discharged, we had to clean the bilges in number two hold. That was one of the worst jobs that we had to undertake. It is such a low restricted space and one can imagine the stench of rotting, fermenting grain. I was staggering.

We would work awhile and emerge as fast as possible and throw up and return and try to continue to work. We were certainly grateful when we completed that job, as it had to be done so the ship could be repaired because wheat burns and the fermenting gases could cause an explosion. After the repairs were completed, we started out in convoy across the North Atlantic. The weather was terrible as usual in the North Atlantic. We pitched and rolled heavily and plowed into the huge waves. Seawater was seeping through the supposedly watertight doors and all the passageways and our rooms were filled with water. As we rolled, the water would slosh around. We had to wear sea boots to go to the toilet or to the mess room to eat. All our clothes got damp. We could not leave anything on the deck in our rooms. We stowed everything we could on the one spare bunk. Even our bedclothes got damp. One cannot imagine how miserable it is to live like that unless one experiences it personally.

The heavy weather in a way was a godsend as it prevented the submarines from attacking us. They rolled and pitched as the water was turbulent at the depth they had to fire their torpedoes at us and our escorts were getting more experienced at attacking them and keeping them away from us. Woe to the ship that developed engine trouble and dropped back or could not keep up with the convoy. They soon became bait for the submarines and were soon sunk. As bad as our conditions were on our ships, we were in awe of the sailors on the corvettes and DE Destroyers. Their living conditions must have been horrifying. They rolled and pitched something awful and I watched them disappearing into a trough. We were all holding our breaths and wondering if they would surface again as they were such small ships. Suddenly, they would pop up again and shake the sea off of them like a bulldog shaking off a dip in a pond. I knew that they were not getting any sleep. They all must have been walking around in a daze. All of us seamen really had deep respect and sympathy for them. They were giving the utmost devotion to duty to protect the convoy so that we could deliver the valuable cargoes that we were carrying. With the sounding of their sirens, they would veer off, charging after a sub that was picked up on their sonar.

After arriving at Lands End, England, the convoy split up as different ships were going to different ports. We were attached to a smaller convoy that was going to ports on the English Channel. We were going to Scotland and our ship was equipped with torpedo nets, a barrage balloon and had a very heavy escort as we would be passing by German-held territory and Germany itself. We were harassed by the German planes and submarines all the way through the English Channel. We finally arrived at Leigh, the port for Edinburgh, Scotland, and started to discharge our cargo of wheat. I often wondered how much of the wheat went into bread and how much found its way into the distillery.

Edinburgh is a very pretty city, dominated by the huge castle of Edinburgh that sits on a very high hill and has a moat surrounding it. The Scots were very friendly to us Americans. They are very different from the English people, not as standoffish as the British. I found them to be more open and much more friendly. I really enjoyed being around the Scots.

The castle was open to visitors but certain areas were closed as there were British troops stationed inside the castle. I enjoyed examining the castle. It was quite a sight to see.

After finishing discharging, we sailed from Leigh, Scotland and were sent on a different route north of Scotland through a passage between the Orkney Islands and the Shetland Islands. What a wildly windy and rough place! The rough seas and currents meet there and produce some of the worst weather you can find anywhere. We were really happy after passing through there, out into the North Atlantic and heading for the States.

The strength of the sea is quite amazing. It can twist and bend and break steel like it was cardboard. All seafarers learned to respect its power, as soon as one has been in a storm at sea.

Can one see the damage it causes aboard a ship? One thinks that the sea is a liquid and cannot possibly damage steel, but it certainly does. I can attest to that fact as I have witnessed a lot of sea damage to a ship in my lifetime.

On one voyage to Cherbourg, France to deliver cargo to the US Army, we were being unloaded by French longshoremen. One day, while working on board the ship, I heard the tramping of feet, the sound of marching men. Out of curiosity, I glanced over on the dock and there was a platoon of SS prisoners guarded by several US Army soldiers. An officer came aboard and had a conference with the Chief Mate, who then called me up to his room and told me to put these SS prisoners to work on board the ship. I did so, having them chip and paint, and I also put them painting the exterior of the ship. I was also ordered to take them at lunchtime to the mess room to be fed. I had a fair knowledge of French so I occasionally spoke with the longshoremen. They knew that I understood French. A delegation of them came to me. They looked ferocious. They said, "You are feeding the prisoners much better than what we can obtain to eat." France was still suffering from destroyed transportation due to the fighting that took place during the invasion.

They pointed out that these men we were feeding were the ones who occupied their territories, murdered them and confiscated all of their food supplies. I pointed out to them that I had no control over this matter as I was only carrying out the orders. I have often wondered who gave the original orders. And why was our ship picked out for this work detail? I have always thought that this was the most distasteful thing I have ever been ordered to do.

In spite of what took place here with the SS prisoners, I did have a chance to make a trip to Paris. I discussed with some US Army guys that I would like to go up and see the city of Paris but I did not know if I could get up to it because the French transportation was still all torn up from the fighting. One of the soldiers said, "I work on the army railroad and you can ride up with us. I will pick you up here at the dock and drive you to the railroad station and you can come aboard the train with me." So, after a while, the twin started up and away we were, on our way to Paris. The train was almost empty. We arrived at Paris and I thanked him for allowing us ride with them. We went and found a hotel room, left our belongings in the room and went off to see the sights of Paris. We were in a very expensive hotel as it was wartime and there were a lot of hotel rooms available. We visited the Eiffel Tower, the Louvre, which did not have too many exhibitions as most of them had been either put back or hid from the Germans. We also visited the Notre Dame Cathedral, Sacred Heart Church, the Arc de Triomphe and, of course, Montmartre, where all of the nightlife is. We visited the nightclubs in the area. After a couple of real busy days and nights, we were ready to return to our ship. Once again, we boarded the US Army train back to Cherbourg, all tired out and broke.

The most joyful feeling I had was on the day when the European war ended. We were in convoy heading for the Mediterranean and one evening we were ordered to turn on our running lights—as the war had ended. What a glorious sight, seeing all the ships with their lights on! US pre-war seamen had not seen this since Pearl Harbor. It indicated one more step towards peace.

We docked at Port Said, Egypt and started unloading our cargo. On a Friday afternoon, I started thinking about going down to Cairo and to see the Pyramids and the Sphinx. So while talking to one of the Army drivers who would be driving some of the cargo down to Cairo, he said to me, "Why don't you ride down with me? I'll give you a ride down." Two other guys and myself rode down with him. The road ran parallel with the Suez Canal and we enjoyed seeing all the sights as we passed through a lot of small villages. We got good insight into life in Egypt. The truck driver dropped us off in front of a hotel that had been sanctioned by the army as a safe place to stay. We were too tired to go anywhere after that long trip and we went to bed early.

The next morning we rose early and found transportation to the Pyramids and spent the day sightseeing and riding camels. One of my companions was the deck maintenance and of Jewish faith. I think that he was a little apprehensive all the time that we were in Egypt and I didn't blame him. I would have, too, if I was Jewish.

We also went to the bazaar and bought some souvenirs and visited the famous Blue Mosque. We had never drunk so much coffee as in every shop we visited we had to drink the coffee the owner offered us. We returned to Port Said via Alexandria. We boarded a train. It was hot and dirty but we enjoyed ourselves in spite of the filth. Egypt is very hot and dirty, loaded with beggars who constantly bother you. Lepers with horrible sores and missing body parts can really turn one off, along with all sorts of cripples with twisted or missing limbs.

The Navy Armed Guard had been removed and shipped home by the USA Air Force so we had some empty quarters.

After discharging our Army cargo, we began to load all sorts of vehicles and artillery. The Army put passengers aboard to be returned home, including two women and some US Army guys. They were quartered in the old Navy quarters. Soon we were on our merrily way home. During the voyage, one of the women and our chief officer became romantically entwined.

As I had to get up to the Chief Mate's room frequently to find out what he wanted me to do about problems that arose, I would find her lying in his berth. Like most voyage romances, it, too, ended when we reached port in the States.

It was a strange happening. I had gone down to Washington, DC from Baltimore as my ship was in the shipyard there. So, I decided to visit the city.

While sitting on a bench in front of the Washington monument, a guy walking down the street looked at me, hurried over to me and said, "Jerry, what are you doing here in Washington?" I then recognized him. He was one of the army personnel we had brought back from Egypt. I guess he, being dressed in civilian clothes, threw me off. He was so glad to see me again. He insisted on showing me around the city of Washington as most seafarers know that we run into each other in all the different seaports in the world.

That was to be my last wartime voyage. While I was on leave from this voyage, the war with Japan ended, but I continued to go to sea as I was a professional seaman.

Chapter IV

THE POST-WAR YEARS

I was going to get a third mate's license during the war, but was discouraged because other people wanted me to give up the sea. I tried to work ashore but I found that the pull of the sea was stronger than my life ashore, so I returned to the life I loved best. I gave up being home constantly with my family and being there for them.

I know that it is hard for people to understand this, but if you would question any seaman, he would tell you the same thing.

I find this almost impossible to explain to anyone. I cannot explain it to myself. Only another seaman can understand this. The plain truth is that seamen are not happy unless they are aboard a ship underway, as they get very restless while being in port.

Often, I reminisce about the crew I sailed with in the pre-war years and about the intellectual conversations that took place in the mess rooms aboard those ships. I soon began to understand the backgrounds of the people involved.

Doctors, lawyers, college professors, schoolteachers, scientists and any profession you can name. Some were escapists, others were alcoholics, and were not following their educational qualifications. It seems that though it was such a waste of talent, they enjoyed going to sea rather than following their chosen professions. If they were happy going to sea, it should not have been anyone's business but their own.

One day, before joining a ship, the company sent me to a doctor for a physical examination as all steamship companies did with new employees.

I was waiting in the doctor's office to be examined. The door opened and there was one of my old shipmates. He said, "Jerry! What are you doing here?" I said, "I am here for a physical to join a ship." "Come in, come in," he said. After I was inside, he pleaded with me not to reveal that I had known him and sailed with him as he told me he had gone back to his medical profession. I told him that I would keep my information about him confidential and never reveal it to anyone. He seemed very happy. He walked me to the door and wished me well on my coming voyage. I was happy to have seen my old friend and shipmate again.

After I studied and took the examination I received a third mate's license and continued sailing. As I sailed on both tankers and freighters, I came to the conclusion that I preferred the tankers as the living conditions were better. I also enjoyed loading and discharging oil cargo better, as on a tanker the whole operation is in your hands.

I also had a lot of incidents that have occurred on ships I was on. I was second mate on one ship and we were on our way to France. As I had been put in charge of first aid aboard this ship, I was on the twelve-to-four watch, which is the second mate's normal watch. As I was passing a passenger ship it started to signal for us to stop. So I called the captain to the bridge and he ordered me to stop the ship, which I did as the wind was very light and the sea was calm. The other ship was of Italian registry. After we stopped, they lowered a lifeboat and came over to our ship and asked about the mutiny we were having aboard our ship. They said they were here to aid us and put it down and we were dumbstruck.

We informed them that we were not having a mutiny aboard. Then, they told us about the radio messages they had received from our radio officer who had transmitted to them that there was a mutiny aboard our vessel and he had barricaded himself into the radio room while the mutineers were breaking down his door.

It seems that this was the start of mental problems for the radio officer. I had to sedate him and keep him sedated all the way to France. After we docked, I took him by taxi to a mental hospital and that was the last I saw of him. It was a great relief to me, as I had to minister to him on my off duty hours. The twelve-to-four watch is the worst watch on board a ship, as one has to get up for meals and other requirements. Your sleeping hours are disturbed quite a bit. It is the most unpopular watch aboard any ship.

I was second mate aboard a liberty ship and we were in a ship-yard getting ready to sail. At 11:30 A.M., I was in the saloon eating dinner before going on watch at 12:00 when one of the crew members stuck his head in the saloon door and informed us that the bosun had just fallen down into number two hold. I rushed out on deck and ran to number two hold and peered down. I saw him lying down on the ship's bottom of the hatch, which, in nautical terms, is called the ceiling. I immediately flew down the ladder, going down to the bottom of the hold. I could see that his skull was split open and blood was oozing out. He was a very powerful man. As he was trying to raise himself up, I had to hold him down. I was also yelling for the shipyard to send down the stretcher basket so that we could put him in it and take him to the hospital. The basket finally arrived and some of the first aid people from the shipyard joined me. We raised him up from the deck, laid him in the basket and strapped him down because he was still trying to move. It seems that the crew was removing dunnage from the cargo hold. Dunnage is lumber that is laid down and cargo is laid on top of it. It is used between cargoes to shore it up.

It seems that he reached over to grab the sling load and pull it over to land it on the main deck. He had reached over too far and lost his balance and fell into the hold, a costly mistake. We sailed on to Galveston, Texas and we were notified by radio that he had died. I became quite upset, as this death could have been prevented by a little caution on his part.

One never gives any thought about having one's citizenship in any nation. The following incident I am going to relate will give the reader a pause to remember. I was on an American export line combination passenger and cargo ship and we were on the Mediterranean run. We sailed from the port of New York and across the North Atlantic to Marseilles, France to Naples, Italy to Livorno, Italy to Genoa, Italy to Pireus, Greece then onto Alexandria, Egypt to Haifa, in what was then Palestine and to Beirut, Lebanon. Then we would make all these ports in reverse order. So, while we were in Marseilles, somebody stowed away and after we sailed, we found this stowaway. It seems that he was a stateless person, had no passport, no identity papers at all. The truth about him came out after a while of questioning. It seems that he was born in Egypt of Italian parents, Egypt would not recognize him as a Egyptian citizen because he was born of Italian parents and Italy would not recognize him because he was born in Egypt. I think his original idea was to stay undiscovered until the ship arrived at Boston, which was our first port of call in the United States. So, on our arrival at Naples, Italy, the ship tried to dump him there but the Italian immigration would not let him land, as he was not considered to be an Italian subject. They then tried to land him at Alexandria, Egypt. The same thing happened.

It would not have been so bad if he had been a genial person but he was a nasty person. He would not work as the company expected him to for his room and board. The ship had a couple of jail cells aboard and that's where he spent most of his time while aboard. It was getting expensive for the ship as they had to hire a guard to watch him in every port that we entered. Finally, after we left Marseilles, France on our return voyage, the ship radioed the agent in Tangiers, Morocco, which is a duty-free port. The agent came out in a boat and met the ship outside of the harbor and he was put into the boat. The agent took him ashore and then told him to get lost. That was the end of a painful experience, for him and for us. There is a large fine if a ship carries an alien into the United States and he gets away from the ship, so the ship must hire guards to watch him for twenty-four hours a day and pray that he does not escape.

One of the most upsetting experiences I have encountered was on a voyage from Houston, Texas to Port Everglades, Florida. My Chief Mate, who had just joined the ship in Houston, was a very personable young man, an exceptionally good tanker man and a very efficient officer.

On the day that we were to arrive at Port Everglades at 3:30 A.M., the twelve-to-four OS knocked on my door and woke me up. He seemed very upset and said, "Captain! Captain! The Chief Mate is dead!" I must have jumped three feet in the air. I said, "What?" He said I just called him to go on watch and when he didn't answer me, I grabbed his foot and shook it and it felt cold. I then turned the light on and saw that he was dead, so I rushed up here to notify you. I hurriedly dressed up and went below. I entered his room and found him lying on his bed with a plastic bag over his head and with a can of ether in his hand. He had evidently brought it aboard with him as I knew that we did not have it in our inventory. I had taken an inventory of our medicine chest only a few days before he had joined the vessel. He evidently had brought it aboard with the intention of committing suicide. What a waste of a fine young life!

It seems that he was having domestic problems. His wife was a professional model and they were living in California. She had thought that she would have more opportunities in New York City so they had moved there. I also found a magazine lying open on his chest. There was a picture of a nude woman on the page and by comparing it with the picture of his wife on his dresser I found that it was the same person.

I had sent a radio message to the company about the suicide and also radioed my agent to set in motion the necessary officials to investigate. There were a lot of them that showed up. The coroner and the US Marshals are the only law enforcement allowed aboard an American ship. The body was finally removed from the ship. I was tied up all day unto late that evening on the official business over this affair. The worst thing I had to do was to talk to his widow. I could not explain to her why he did it. I and some of my other officers had searched his room for a suicide note and never found one. Months later, a relief chief mate searching for something in the filing cabinet came across it and brought it up to my office. I told him about the incident and told him how we had searched for it. He had inserted it with some cargo papers. That is why it was not found. The only enjoyment I had that day was when an old shipmate who had retired and was living in Fort Lauderdale came over and visited me. I supposed it must have been in the papers. I was very happy to see him as I had not seen him since he had retired. It sure was a diversion from what I had been going through that day as I did not even have a chance to go uptown. Even to this day, I think about this event.

I have had some strange tasks to perform while on board some ships, but the one I am going to relate is very strange. I was on board a ship owned by an old, wealthy family who owned a lumber company and a steamship company. It seems that they had a juvenile delinquent who was causing them a tremendous amount of problems. One of them came up with what they thought was the answer to their problem—put him aboard one of their ships. They thought that the discipline and confinement might straighten him out. I said, "Now I am going to have to be a jailer and a counselor too." They must have cleared this up and got the permission of seamen's union, as I don't think the union would have dared to refuse them.

When he first came on board, he was a little on the nasty side so I took him into my office and laid down the law to him. I also read the maritime law on disobedience. If he disobeyed any orders given to him, he could be shackled and fed only bread and water as long as the disobedience lasted, and the loss of wages of three or four days' pay for each day of disobedience added up as well. Well, my action worked. I also told him that being the owner's son didn't mean a thing aboard my ship as I was the ship's master and my word was law.

Then, after that, I guess he thought it over and a complete change came over him. He turned out to be a very polite and conscientious young man, but I was sure glad to finally put him ashore and send him back to his parents.

I guess the most shocking experience that I have had in my seagoing life was the grounding of my ship by the third mate. We were on a return trip to Houston, Texas from Providence, Rhode Island.

After departing from Brenton Reef Light, one takes a direct course to the Cape Hatteras Light and then to Bimini Shoal Light and when abeam, sets a course for the Florida Coast to Jupiter Lighthouse and then runs along the coast of Florida, running about a mile-and-a-half off of the reefs, constantly changing courses between navigational points. I am always on the bridge when approaching shoals, reefs or land. I was on the bridge long before we approached Bimini Shoal. After changing course to bring us about two miles off of Jupiter Lighthouse, I went below and left orders with the third mate to call me if any problems arose and also notify me when the ship was about ten miles off of Jupiter Lighthouse. After receiving a call from him telling me we were about ten miles off of the lighthouse, I went up on the ship's bridge and studied the chart and the cross bearings he had laid down on the chart that showed the ship's position, as cross bearings are the most accurate positions in navigation. One takes a bearing on two or more land positions, normally lighthouse on and buoys which have a known position.

The third mate evidently took bearings, but laid down the bearings on the wrong lights, giving us a false position as this mate had been aboard the ship for a while before I assumed command. I had thought that he was a capable and competent officer. I stayed on the bridge until we came abeam the next lighthouse and watched him change to the next course to bring the ship abeam the next lighthouse. I then left the bridge and went below, not finding any reason to become suspicious of his navigation. As I was watching television in the ship's lounge, I began to get a little uneasy. Why, I can't tell you. I glanced out a few times and I saw ships passing us by the port side when they should be passing on the starboard side. I went up to the bridge and there was this crunching sound and the ship shook and vibrated. I instantly knew that the ship had run aground. What a shock as a ship's captain! That was the worst thing that could happen to me.

I arrived on the bridge in a matter of seconds and found that we were aground on Mollasses Reef. I still, to this day, cannot imagine how any officer could do this as the ship was seen to be heading right for the light and common sense would have told you were too close.

I was in a state of shock. If I ever considered mayhem on someone, I considered performing it on him. I tried to work the ship off the reef by working the engine and the ship's rudder but to no avail. I then radioed the company and they arranged for a salvage company to haul us off of the reef, as the hull was punched and also the pump room. With the aid of tugboats, they hauled us off of the reef and we anchored. A diver came aboard and I directed him to valves. He would have to open them to close, in order to pump out the cargo tanks and the pump room that had been flooded. In the meanwhile, divers were plugging the holes in the hull with wooden plugs. After the holes were plugged, we started the cargo pumps and the bilge pump in the pump room. Soon we were successful in drying the ship up.

As I had notified the company that the closest shipyard was Tampa, Florida, I then proceeded to Tampa. We docked. After arrival, the company arranged to have the ship dry-docked to inspect the hull. We had to clean the cargo tanks before entering the shipyard. So, a barge was hired and brought alongside so that the washing could be pumped into the barge. A tanker's tanks are cleaned by using high-pressure hoses hooked to a *Butterworth* machine, which has nozzles and a small water turbine that turns the machine 360 degrees in two directions.

The seawater is heated to about 200 degrees to force the oil off the bulkheads in the tanks and has about 150 pressures. This has been the most successful method found to clean petroleum out of cargo tanks.

After we finished cleaning and gas freeing the cargo tanks, we entered the dry dock. After inspecting the ship's hull and the ship's age, the company decided that it would not be economical to repair her and the decision was made to scrap her. We shifted back to a dock and I paid off the crew. The company asked me to stay aboard and remove equipment and navigable equipment that could be used on other ships that were owned by the company.

I rented a truck and picked up laborers on a street corner where they gathered every day to be hired. I put them to work removing equipment. I would also go and buy them sandwiches and soda every day and I paid them every day.

I had asked the company what they wanted to do with the food stores. They told me to give it to some charity. There was a Catholic orphanage in Tampa. I called them and asked if they wanted the food. They said they would be grateful. I also told them they would have to come and remove the food. They received quite a lot of food. I stayed with the ship until everything that was useable was removed. I was informed by the company that I could have anything that I wanted but, foolishly, I didn't take certain items that I now wish I had taken. I had now ended my sojourn as employer, paymaster and caterer.

I also had to face a Coastguard Board of Inquiry and was found not at fault and cleared. I then returned home and in a matter of days I was on board another ship as master again for the same company.

One of the more interesting jobs I had was delivering oceano-graphic research ships from the Marinette Ship in Marinette, Wisconsin to the Navy Yard at Boston, Ma.

I was home on vacation when my union called me and asked if I would take the job as the shipyard was having problems securing a qualified ship's master. They also said that I could extend my vacation by the number of days I would be employed by the shipyard. I agreed to take on the delivering job and flew up to Green Bay with two mates from my local union. We were put up in a motel for the night in Marinette. The next morning, we joined the ship in the shipyard and the coastguard came on board to check our licenses to make sure we were qualified. They also asked me as to why I did not send a photocopy of my license to them. I carefully pointed out to them that Federal Law prohibits any copy of a license. It seems to me that they should have been more informed about that. Well, I had a few very busy days getting the ship ready to sail. The local newspaper sent a reporter and photographer down to the ship to interview me and asked me various questions about how the coming voyage would proceed and any problems that could occur. I told them we had a crew of professional seafarers so we would not have any problems handling the vessel. Away we sailed via the Great Lakes seaway through all the ships' locks into the St. Lawrence River out to the North Atlantic Ocean and down to the port of Boston, Massachusets. The crew had easily fallen into shipboard routine. It was a very pleasant voyage and we did not encounter any large problems.

After delivering the ship, the next day I flew up to Green Bay again and over to Marinette again to take the next vessel to Boston. I then found out that my picture and story had been put on the front page of the newspaper. The only change in this trip was the fact that we had taken some passengers on board, who were oceanographers and marine scientists. Why, I did not know. I started out this voyage with about the same crew because they were a good and pleasant group and professional. One day, as we were passing through some of the locks, I could hear some voices and I looked around to see where they were coming from. Lo and behold, they were up on the radar mast right in front of the radar antenna. I was so shocked that I could not talk for a moment and then I blew my stack. "You dumb bastards! Get down from there right now!" After they got down on the bridge deck, I read them the riot act. I said, "You are supposed to be educated but you are downright fools. If I had not heard your voices, I could have turned on the radar and fried you to death. Don't you ever do a stupid thing like that again, or I will put you at the next lock we come to." This stupid act really had shaken me up, when I thought of what could have happened to them.

I have made a few other trips up the St. Lawrence River through Seaway Locks and up through the Great Lakes with tankers to pick up a load of wheat. Somebody came up with that idea, which was a good one because on freighters and bulk carriers shifting boards must be installed which are usually composed of wood and built from the holds' ceiling, or bottom, as landlubbers would say. It can be quite expensive but very necessary as it prevents the grain from shifting in a storm and can cause the ship to tip over or even turn over. That has happened in the past. It taught us a very valuable lesson. Tankers are compartmentalized. As the cargo tanks have bulkheads, the grain cannot shift in the tanks and as such shifting boards are not needed.

Since we have been mentioning the Great Lakes, it would now be the time to include a little information about our brothers in the Great Lakes Shipping. As we saltiest call them sweet water sailors, they sail on fresh water almost all of the time. Some of the Great Lakes ships were sent out to sail on the ocean during World War II, as the German Submarines wrecked havoc with our ocean-going fleet. At the beginning of the war, we could not replace the amount of ship losses. A lot of Great Lakes sailors shifted over to deep sea ships and, to this day, you have men who shift back and forth from Lakes to ocean and vice versa. Great Lakes vessels last much longer than a saltwater vessel because a chemical reaction called electrolysis takes place in salt water and ocean-going ships have anodes placed around the hull to offset this. More are placed around the rudder post and stern as the electrolysis is greater there because of the bronze propeller creating an even greater reaction. A lot of tanker companies tried to reduce the electrolysis in the cargo tanks by installing anodes in the cargo tanks but I don't think it was too successful in the long run. As the commercial life of an ocean-going vessel is about twenty years, in comparison there have been Great Lakes vessels in operation for fifty and sixty years. Electrolysis does not take place in fresh water.

The largest amount of shipping in the Great Lakes has been the large bulk carriers hauling iron ore and limestone to the huge steel mills around the Lakes. They also carried stone, sand, cement, wheat and other grains. There are also a lot of self-unloaders on the Lakes. In comparison, there are only a few self-unloaders in the ocean-going trade, mostly coal colliers running coastwise. The Lake trade is just as hazardous as their counterparts in the saltwater trade. They do not make long voyages like us seafarers make, but they are constantly on the move from one port to another and have to keep passing through locks from one Lake to another. The only respite they have is when the ships are laid up because the Lakes are impassable during some of the winter months. Some of the tankers operate all year long, as petroleum is a necessity in that heavily populated area.

Basically, they have the same crew but some in the deck department are called wheelsman, watchman and deck man but perform the same duties. The engine department is called the same as for seagoing oilers, firemen, wipers and Chief First Assistant, second Assistant and third Assistant as well as engineers, stewards' cooks and mess man. There is a difference in the deck officers, as their licenses are limited to Great Lakes unless they have sailed on the oceans, but all the Great Lakes masters and mates also have pilot's endorsements. Compared to deep-sea masters and mates, they have unlimited licenses to carry any tonnage to any oceans. So we do not intrude on each other's industries but, in my lifetime, I have rarely seen men who have had both licenses. But there have been some who have gone from Lakes to ocean and vice versa. Some of the seamen still do so. The Great Lakes have had some great storms and a lot of casualties, sinkings and groundings over the years, so even being close to shore is no guarantee of safety as traveling on water—salt or fresh—is hazardous at best.

One of the biggest deceptions ever foisted on the American public was the necessity of the St. Lawrence Seaway. The public was told that it was for the purpose of allowing ocean-going vessels to transit the Great Lakes but in reality it was for the large steel mills vessels to be able to transit the Great Lakes to bring iron ore from the mines in Labrador to their steel mills because the mines in Minnesota had petered out. So the American public was conned into building the seaway locks for the benefit and use of the big steel companies.

My last voyage on a liberty ship was certainly a nerve-wracking one for me. The company I was working for had both tankers and freighters, so they asked me if I would take this ship for one voyage as it was almost ready to sail from Louisiana for Calcutta, India with a full load of wheat. I flew down to New Orleans and got aboard the ship one afternoon and sailed the next day. I sailed to Free Port, Bahamas to pick up fuel oil as a seagoing ship sinks deeper in fresh water than it does in salt water. After taking my bunkers, I sailed for North Africa and the port of Tangiers. After loading bunkers and fresh water, I continued my voyage towards the Suez Canal. I transited the Suez Canal after clearing the canal and entering the Red Sea. The engine room called and asked if I would stop the ship as they needed to make some adjustments to the shaft. It happened to be a bad place to stop. I told them to keep the engines going until I found a safe place to anchor. I proceeded down the Red Sea until I found a safe place to anchor and I did so. At the completion of the repairs, I again proceeded down through the Red Sea to the port of Debouti, Somaliland to again bunker the ship. It is a long haul to Calcutta, India via the Island of Ceylon and up the Bay of Bengal so I took enough fuel to have enough in case of a bad storm. After rounding the Horn of Africa, I laid a course for Ceylon. As we were proceeding on course, I received another call from the engine room notifying me that we could not continue as the shaft had split in half. So I let the ship drift while keeping the depth finder operating until I found a place where it was shallow enough to anchor the ship. When I found a spot shallow enough to anchor, it was south of an Island of the Horn of Africa. I notified the company and received an answer telling me they had ordered a salvage tug from the Persian Gulf to tow the ship to Bombay, India. In the meantime, I had a crew member come down with mental illness so bad that I had to handcuff him to the bunk in the ship's hospital. I had left written orders on the ship's bridge to continue to take bearings on the island and notify me if they changed. One day, I was down in the hospital tending to the ill seaman when a member of the deck department found me and said, "The mate wants you on the bridge right away. The ship is drifting." I immediately sent the Chief Mate forward to check on the anchor. He engaged the windlass and began to haul up the anchor until the chain's end, which had no anchor on it. The anchor chain had parted. I had him drop the starboard anchor and it finally held. But after a few days, the wind picked up and we commenced, dragging our anchor and getting closer to the island all the time. I feared that the wind would drive the ship right into the islands' cliffs and that the ship would break up. So I took my mental patient up on the ship's bridge and handcuffed him to one of the handrails on the bridge and gave the handcuff key to the mate on watch.

I then sounded the general alarm to get everybody out on deck to save the ship. I put some of the crew to swing out the ship's lifeboats in order to abandon ship if we had to.

I had some of the engine crew bring up torch to burn away the clamps holding the spare anchor on the deckhouse at number two hatch. In the meantime, I had the deck department raise the booms at number two hatch. While they were topping the booms, I had others hauling the anchor chain back to number two hatch outside of the ship's hull and pulled some of the chain on deck and lashed to a pad eye on the bulk ward. We connected the anchor to the chain after lifting it with the cargo runner.

We then lifted the anchor with the cargo runner and lowered it over the side until the rope lashing held the anchor and chain. Then we disconnected the cargo runner from the anchor and cut the rope lashing holding the anchor and chain. Away went the anchor and it began holding ground. We now had two anchors down and I prayed that they would hold to keep us off the island until the salvage tug arrived. We kept in touch with the salvage tug until she arrived. She immediately began to hook us up and started heaving us away from that island and towards Bombay. What a relief and joy I found after that ordeal! It took about nineteen days to tow us to Bombay. They were going to put the ship at anchor outside the harbor, but I had a good friend in Bombay who happened to be the harbormaster. I had known him for a few years and we had become close friends. I used to be invited to dinner at his house quite often.

I received quite a shock one day. We had been discharging our wheat cargo, which was donated to India from the United States, the discharged wheat was being bagged on the dock. One day, out of curiosity, I walked on the dock and through the warehouse to the deck on the other side and lo and behold there was a Russian ship loading the wheat we were discharging! That is what happened to the wheat that was not to be sold and was to feed the people of India. The crew and I were flown home as they we were putting a new section of shaft on board the ship. I believed that the ship was sold to some foreign owners.

As I continued my seagoing career, I could see changes that would affect the industry. The break bulk system of loading ships was changing. First, the loading of freighters is done mostly in the companies' offices. A lot of planning takes place as cargo must be stowed according to what port is the first stop. One cannot stow such cargo in the lower hold as one would have to unload tons just to discharge that cargo. Normally, that space is used to load cargo for the return voyage. There are other factors involved, such as draft. One wants a ship's draft with the stern lower than the bow and with no list port or starboard. Also, one must not have a sagging or hogging factor so it does not put a strain on the vessel hull, which could cause the ship to break. Today, they have computers to do all those calculations.

The first thing I noticed was that shippers began using steel containers welded shut so as to prevent pillage, or stealing, as shore people would say. It also cut down on the handling of cargo. That was one of the biggest problems as the cargo was unloaded from the trucks on the docks onto pallets. The pallets were then loaded on board in the various holds and were handled by the longshoremen and stacked in the hold in various places. That is where the pillage happened. That is why shippers devised the steel boxes and the whole shipment could be unloaded onto a truck and be delivered safely in one container. It sure saved the insurance company money.

The next innovation I came across was when I shipped aboard a tanker, which I thought to be a common tanker. When I was boarding her, I had noticed that she had some sort of a deck placed above her main deck. It certainly looked odd as she had been discharging at an oil company dock. So I thought no more about it as the ship was waiting for me to join her to sail. I also remember that it was still snowing when I joined her. I had to walk through snow that came up to my chest. I almost turned around and went back home because of the height of the snow and the trouble I had walking through it.

I soon found out what the additional deck was for. I was told the deck was for carrying the trailer box of a trailer truck. The platform or deck had holes in it. The box had legs that fitted through the platform and after the box was landed, a wedge was driven through the leg and a toggle pin was inserted to keep the wedge from working out. This ship was the second tanker that McLean had purchased to commence his shipping line he called sea land. This was a man who knew absolutely nothing about ships but knew trucking as he owned a large trucking company. He was a visionary who had this conception of carrying truck trailers on a ship, putting them ashore and hooking up the tractors to them and delivering them right to their destination without the cargo being handled. He revolutionized the shipping industry and everyone was copying him. Most of the dry cargo of the world is now moved in this manner. The original ships were very bad on the crew. After entering port, we would go to an oil dock, load an oil cargo on the Houston end and then shift to a cargo dock and start discharging and loading the boxes on one side of the ship. Then, all hands had to turn the ship around and load and discharge the rest of the boxes. Then, we would sail for Seawarren, New Jersey and do the reverse because discharging the oil first made the ship too high for the cranes to handle the boxes. I met McLean once as he made a southbound trip with us and he was trying to sell his stock to the ship's officers. I did not buy any stock as I did not think that his company would be successful.

Boy, was I wrong! I guess I was too set in the old ways of the sea.

I also got involved in the Vietnam War. The ship I was master on was chartered to the Military Sealift Command, or MSC, as it is known. All the time I was on her, we spent our time carrying jet fuel, av gas and motor gas into Vietnam from various ports such as Saudi Arabia, Bahrain, Iran, Subic Bay, Philippines, Okinawa and Japan. Most of the ports I discharged at in Vietnam were Chu Li, China Beach, Da Nang, etc.

A few times we really ran into some hostile action. One night, after arriving off the port of Chu Li, I was conning the ship into port. Suddenly, all hell broke loose. The Vietcong started to attack the base, which had an airfield. The hillsides had erupted to the sounds and flashes of artillery and mortars. Shells came flying towards the ship. At that time I think we were a little too far off for the Vietcong to hit the ship. About the same time, my radar conked out, causing me more problems. Fortunately, I was able to bring the ship invisibly as it was a very dark night with no moonlight to help me. When daylight came, I brought the ship to the buoy and tied up and heaved up the submarine cargo line. While we were discharging our cargo, the Vietcong were still dropping mortar shells onto the airport's landing strip but our planes continued to take off and land all during the time we were discharging our cargo of jet fuel and av gas. I was certainly not disappointed to leave Chu Li and the Vietcong behind and sail away to more peaceful waters.

Another incident happened in Da Nang harbor. I had tied up to a buoy bow first and then heaved up the submarine hose to discharge into. While we were discharging our cargo, somebody noticed a boat at the mooring buoy with some Vietcong trying to cut our mooring lines with axes. I thought of trying to discourage them by turning the ship's searchlight on them. The army had sent a couple of GIs on board as guards, but they did not bring their weapons with them. A lot of help they were! Finally, we contacted the harbor control and they sent an armed patrol out to attack them and drove them off. You can bet the following night the GIs had their weapons with them.

About that time, I came to the conclusion that war is for the young. What was a middle-aged guy like me doing here?

In the years just before I retired, I began to see changes taking place in the maritime industry and it foretold what was coming. The steamship companies were committed to reducing their crew sizes. It was not only the cost of wages but also increasing cost of pension and medical benefits. They began to seek other ways to reduce the cost. One of the first things I noticed was the installation of dishwashers on board the ships, thus reducing the crew to one man, the pantry man. The next change was combining the chief steward and chief cook to a one-man job and also eliminating the third cook. Then, the boilers were automated. Thus, three more men were eliminated. As newer ships were built, the engine rooms were completely automated with complete bridge control, which, I think, is a great improvement.

As the time element is important when one rings the telegraph, it must be answered by the engineer on watch. He answers the telegraph order and grabs the engine throttle to slow, advance or reverse the engine. If he is away from his station working at a repair job that is necessary, time is lost while he leaves the job he is working on and comes and answers the telegraph. While reducing the crew size, they were increasing the size of ships, thus carrying several times more cargo with reduced size crews. The *T2 Tanker* built during the war was from a pre-war Standard Oil design and was the backbone of the oil industry for years. It was of ten thousand tons and the industry began to build them bigger and bigger. The first was a thirty thousand one. Then, fifty and finally, one hundred thousand tons and up to one thousand feet long, but the large ships with their deep draft could not get into load and discharge in a lot of the world's ports. So they came up with new tactics, like they did in the Persian Gulf. They ran submarine hoses of eighteen and twenty-four diameter on the ocean floor and mooring buoys for the ships to tie up to the water sufficiently deep, so the ship does not touch bottom.

On the discharging end, they find an anchorage that is deep enough so that they can have barges and/or smaller ships to come alongside to lighten up the supertanker in order that it can dock where there is insufficient water. For a full load the container ships are also getting larger and larger.

Ships keep getting larger and the turnaround is also getting faster. Tankers were always considered the fast turnaround, staying in port twenty to thirty hours but that at least gave crew members time to spend a little time ashore and time to be at home if they had entered a port near their home. But now the container ships have beaten that time by a twelve-hour turnaround time, which is hard on the crew.

The maritime industry also has a problem. We have a Merchant Marine Academy at Kings Point, New York that is turning out merchant marine officers. The States Maine, Massachusetts, New York, Pennsylvania, Texas and California also have academies that graduate ship officers each year for an industry that cannot absorb them.

The shipping industry has gone from the largest in the world after World War II to almost the bottom as we now only have about five hundred ships under the American flag, which is a disgrace to the most powerful nation on earth.

Americans graduating from these academies must seek employment on foreign ships at lower wages in order to work at their trade. This has happened time and again. But each time our nation gets into a conflict somewhere in the world, it calls on us to provide the ships and men and we respond, as always. But we cannot build a fleet of ships overnight and train crew instantly. The frustration the men who have just graduated from these schools face must be great. I know the frustration of not being able to work in a chosen industry as I had to retire due to developing a bad case of diabetes. It really affected me mentally and physically as I was not as happy ashore as I had been sailing.

One of the most touching experiences that I ever had in my years of going to sea was on a coastwise trip from Houston, Texas to Fall River, Massachusetts. We were riding the Gulf Stream northward off of the coast of Florida and close to Miami, Florida when the lookout on the ship's bow reported a light off of the starboard bow. I was called to the bridge by the second mate. As we approached closer, we could make out people waving so I slowed down the ship and approached what turned out to be a raft made up of four inner tubes lashed together with burlap on top of them. I brought the ship alongside of them and stopped the vessel. It turned out to be seven Cubans. They were all related as husband and wife and cousins. A seven-year-old boy seemed to be in the worst condition as the burlap on the inner tube he was riding on had deteriorated and his lower body was hanging in the water and he held on with his arms. The wave action caused his body to go up and down and his hips were rubbed raw. He was in a pitiful condition. They had left Cuba outside of Havana twelve days before with a little food, water and milk for their eleven-month-old baby. Surprisingly, the baby was in excellent condition. They were all in a poor state with raw patches on their bodies and terribly sunburnt and dehydrated. We got them on board. In the meantime, we were in contact with the coastguard. They directed us to meet them off the Miami sea buoy. We put them in the ship's hospital, which has the only bathtub on the ship. I had them all take baths to remove the salt that was encrusted on their bodies. While helping them aboard our vessel, they screamed when we touched them to help them aboard. After they had bathed, all of the crew donated clothes to them, including myself, and we fed them as they hadn't eaten for days, except the baby who had milk every day and was in good shape because it was well taken care of. They tried to give us what little money they had in an old tobacco can. They were taken off my ship by the coastguard and brought into Miami. As we had some Spanish-speaking crew members on board, I used one as an interpreter and asked them why they undertook such a dangerous voyage. The woman told me that she could not raise children under a communist regime.

When we found them, they were on the fringe of the Gulf Stream. If we had missed them, they would surely have perished as they were out of the shipping lanes. I think of them often and wonder how they made out as their names were kept secret because of their relatives back in Cuba.

One of the strangest disappearances I have come across was on a voyage from Houston, Texas to Pakistan with a load of wheat while passing through the Bahamas Islands on a passage known to us seamen as the hole in the wall. As the Bahamas stretch from north of Cuba to the center of Florida, this is the easiest passage for a vessel heading for the Mediterranean and the Suez Canal. While passing through the hole in the wall, I was up on the bridge and I noticed the twelve-to-four third assistant engineer walking up the foredeck and going into the forecastle. I remarked to the third mate on watch, What is the third assistant doing up in the forecastle. He then told me that the chief engineer had asked him to do a job for him. He was going up to look for some wood in the forecastle.

The weather was bright and sunny with a wind force of four or five with a flowing sea, which caused a light wave to come aboard the main deck occasionally but not sufficiently enough to wash a man overboard. Suddenly, the bridge phone rang. It was someone on the after poop deck all excited, saying they just passed the third assistant engineer and he was in the sea shouting for help. We immediately turned the ship around with almost all of the crew searching the sea to see if they could spot him. We also notified the coastguard. We searched for hours but to our great dismay failed to find him.

How did he fall into the sea? We never found out as the ship was loaded and we were not rolling or pitching and we were not having waves aboard strong enough to wash a man overboard. It has been a mystery to me since then and I am still puzzled whenever I think of it.

The sea is a dangerous environment for a human being as it is full of predators ready to attack. There are sharks, and sea snakes whose bite is fatal. They are related to the cobra. There are also barracudas waiting to tear a chunk of flesh off you should you enter into their domain. I have seen parts of the oceans that just teem with these creatures like the Gulf of Panama on the Pacific side of the canal and the northwestern coast of Colombia. The sharks and sea snakes just abound there. I have noticed them all across the Pacific Ocean. I have seen sea snakes and sharks in the Red Sea and Persian Gulf. One of the main industries in that area is pearl harvesting. I had spoken to inhabitants of that area and inquired about the dangers of diving. Did they have casualties? They said, "Of course, but that is the risk they have to take."

On one trip after we had discharged part of our cargo at Pearl Harbor, we were on our way to discharge the rest of our cargo of jet fuel at Guam. A bearing on the engine shaft burned out. As we had a spare one on board, the engineers were going to replace the burnt-out one with the spare one because we could not proceed with a burnt bearing. We began drifting. At that time, we were off of the French Frigate Shoals, which are a continuation of the Hawaiian Islands that continue to the West not Islands. The coral reefs were teeming with sharks. Some of the crew members were catching them with meat hooks that the chief steward had loaned them from the meat locker. They were baiting the hooks with chunks of scrap meat and when they caught one, they would haul it aboard with the deck winch. It was an effort to kill the shark after it was hauled on board. A couple of seamen worked for hours, cutting into it to kill it. Just when they thought it was dead, it would revive and start snapping with its huge jaws and at times somebody jumped away just in time to escape being bitten.

One day, I came out on the boat deck and saw some of the crew swimming in the sea. They had put over a pilot's ladder and had entered the water. I started yelling at them as I could see sharks swimming around not too far away. When they heard the word shark, they soon scrambled out of the water. When you are swimming you are at sea level and cannot see around. As I was standing on the boat deck and I was about twenty feet higher than they were, I could see the shark fins moving through the water. They were sure lucky that no one had been bitten.

I strongly disagree with marine biologists who claim that sharks will not attack you in the water. If you are in the water and they are hungry, as they always seem to be, they will attack you and eat you if you are near to them. I have observed this for years from the deck of a ship. The Malacca Straits is another place full of sharks. In fact, most tropical waters are dangerous for humans as they abound with sharks and sea snakes.

Man has always been attracted to and fascinated by the sea. Is it some prehistoric biological urge that we have carried with us from pre-historical times? I often wonder, as we go back to sea time and time again.

Man has traveled on the sea since he first learned to construct a craft that would float to propel himself some distance on the surface of water and then construct a craft that could carry him and some goods that he could trade for other materials, which he needed.

In spite of the drastic conditions that they have lived under from ancient times to the excellent condition of today's vessels with the fast turnaround, they return time and time again. We wonder why we do it in spite of it all. It must be something in our primitive makeup.

Chapter V

LAMENTS OF AN OLD SEAFARER

Why do I find myself stranded here in this dry and desolate land so far from the ocean that I loved so much?

I feel like a beached whale that finds itself out of its environment and longs to return to it.

How I miss the clean fresh sea breezes and the feel of the ship's movements under me.

I miss the ever-changing sky and seas that show a different face each day.

There is a longing in me to watch the great whales basking in the sun on a calm day and dolphins racing in from all directions to play in our bows wash and then scoot off, never to be seen again.

I miss the horizon that stretches out for miles around you and a vast quiet, occasionally punctured by the raucous squawking of sea gulls as we approach land.

I even miss the fury of violent storms that smash tremendous waves over us and keep our ship awash and plunging and rolling heavily.

The occasional sighting of vicious sharks and deathly sea snakes swimming by and the huge manta rays flinging their bodies out of the water and landing again with a loud boom.

The night watches that are so quiet and reflective and you gaze at the sky ablaze with planets, stars and occasionally see a shooting star that stretches from horizon to horizon.

All that is heard during the night is the wind in the ship's rigging and the muffled sounds of the ship's engines propelling us towards our destination with our cargo.

I can only relive my past life in memories and thoughts. The sea beckons to me, but I cannot answer her call.

If I could shed this old worn out and pain-filled body.

What has happened to that young, strong and vigorous body

that I once possessed?

All that is left are dreams and memories. If only I could return to my beloved sea.

Made in United States
North Haven, CT
09 April 2022

18064548R00054